A CAPSULE HISTORY OF BAPTISTS

FINANCIAL COSPONSORS

WHO MADE THIS PUBLICATION POSSIBLE

Cooperative Baptist Fellowship of Georgia

Cooperative Baptist Fellowship of North Carolina

The National Cooperative Baptist Fellowship

Cooperative Baptist Fellowship of Louisiana

Cooperative Baptist Fellowship of South Carolina

North Central Region, Cooperative Baptist Fellowship

Mid-Atlantic Cooperative Baptist Fellowship

Cooperating Baptist Fellowship of Oklahoma

Baptist Fellowship of Northeast

Tennessee Cooperative Baptist Fellowship

DEDICATION

To a new generation of Baptists,

upon whom falls the task of

knowing,

teaching,

and living

the Baptist witness

in Baptists' fifth century

A CAPSULE HISTORY
OF BAPTISTS

BRUCE T. GOURLEY

Baptist History and Heritage Society
Atlanta, Georgia
2010

Copyright 2010

Baptist History and Heritage Society

Atlanta, Georgia

Printed in the United States of America
Library of Congress Control Number: 2009941890
ISBN: 978-1-57843-066-6

Liz Gibson, Designer

Baptist History and Heritage Society
3001 Mercer University Drive
Atlanta, Georgia 30341
678-547-6095

CONTENTS

PREFACE

Although raised in a Baptist church, I knew little about the story of my own faith until my college years. And although four centuries of Baptist faith have produced a rich library of literature concerning the heritage, beliefs, and individuals that comprise the Baptist story, too many Baptists do not know the story, while even the most informed know that there is always much more to be learned.

This volume, accordingly, can serve as a guidebook along the highway of the Baptist pilgrimage. Briefly sketching the general contours of the first four hundred years of Baptist life and thought, it is intended for general use by those within and without the Baptist faith.

For the reader seeking an introduction to Baptists, this short book provides an easy-to-read entry point into the Baptist narrative and provides guidance for further reading and research. In addition, the reader who is seeking an enhanced understanding of the people called Baptists will hopefully find helpful themes and newly-discovered persons that collectively contribute to a more robust Baptist portrait. And well-versed readers, the author wishes to believe, may discern within this slender volume a refreshing rewording of the broad Baptist trajectory, as well as timely historical analysis.

Freedom is the central theme of this narrative. From their earliest days, Baptists stood apart from most other Christian groups because of a firm commitment to individual freedom of conscience, congregational autonomy, religious liberty, and separation of church and state. This central motif of voluntary, non-coerced faith emanated from Baptists' experience with the Christ of scripture, and contrasted with a longtime, widespread religious understanding of faith expressed in infant baptism, ecclesial edicts, and creedal conformity.

The Baptist story is one of a tiny sect whose faith-in-action shook theological and political foundations worldwide. Courageous individuals, persecuted believers, nation-shaping ideas, theological and ideological divisions, embattled visions, periods of exodus, renewal movements, and geographical transformation characterized Baptist developments. Against this backdrop, Baptists' commitment to their founding principles surged and ebbed throughout the past four centuries, subject to a myriad of pressures from both within and without, but never fading away. Growing in complexity with the passing of time, the Baptist story offers insights into early twenty-first-century Christian faith at large, and contemporary Baptist identity in particular.

This capsule history flows better by placing all notes at the back of the book. A general notes section serves as a starting point for further research. Specific notes for each chapter then follow. Thus, the notes contain general guidelines for further research, and specific suggestions of volumes in which movements, themes, and individuals are fleshed out to a much greater degree than allowed within this volume.

In the end, if this volume leads the reader further down the road of understanding the people called Baptists, it will have served its purpose.

ONE

FREEDOM FIGHTERS
1609-1791

Prison bars and hostile courts on two
continents during the seventeenth and
eighteenth centuries fueled freedom
movements unlike any the world had ever
known: the liberation of human conscience
and the separation of church and state.
Political and religious authorities in
Britain tried mightily to repress the little
religious sect that refused to be silenced.

Theocrats in the colonies sought to eradicate the troublesome dissenters from the New World. The religious and political establishment, in short, denied earthly citizenship and shut the gates of heaven in order to silence dissident cries for freedom. And yet, the small, persecuted sect that came to be known as Baptists persevered.

Against all odds, the freedom fighters slowly, relentlessly gnawed the cords that had bound human conscience for over twelve hundred years. They endured death, beatings, whippings, and stonings. Surging from dank jails, back alleys, and dark forests, the Baptist cry for freedom perplexed the powerful and inspired other dissenters.

From their beginnings, Baptists were the subject of an eradication campaign directed by the most powerful figures in England. Thomas Helwys (c. 1575-1616), a wealthy and respected layman who cast his lot with the first Baptist congregation in 1609 in Amsterdam, was jailed in 1612 in Newgate, the most loathsome and feared prison in England. Within four years of his incarceration, at about the age of forty, Helwys became the first Baptist martyr. The story of his faith and death defined the narrative of the people called Baptists until the late eighteenth century, while his personal convictions grounded the Baptist nexus and ethos for over four centuries.

THOMAS HELWYS
MARTYR AND DEFINER OF THE FAITH

Born into a wealthy family of Norman descent that owned vast tracts of land throughout England, Thomas Helwys was schooled in law. As a young man, however, he gravitated toward dissenters from the Church of England, questioning church authority over the lives of citizens. Joining a Separatist congregation led by John Smyth (c. 1570-1612) in Gainsborough, Lincolnshire, Helwys cast his lot with dissenters who believed that pure religion could only be obtained by making a clean break from the Church of England.

Separatists, in short, were convinced that the Church of England, having split from the Roman Catholic Church in 1531, remained fundamentally corrupt (Puritans, by contrast, also criticized the Church of England, but chose to remain within the church and seek reform).

Harassed and threatened by the state church, the Gainsborough Separatist congregation fled to Amsterdam in the winter of 1607/08 to escape a possible death sentence from the king and church. Believing they would be safe, Helwys's family remained in England. But his wife, Joan, refused to pledge allegiance to the Church of England and was cast into prison for three months, and afterwards banished from the country.

By the time of his forced migration, Helwys stood as a recognized lay leader within the little fellowship, to the point that history remembers the exiled body of some forty believers as the Smyth-Helwys congregation. Smyth, a former Anglican priest, is widely considered the founding father of Baptists. While in exile in Holland in 1609, Smyth rejected his heritage of infant baptism and taught believer's baptism to his followers. At this point, his break with Anglicanism reached completion, for the foundation of the Church of England rested upon the act of infant baptism by which new members were added to both the rolls of the church and the scrolls of heaven.

For Smyth, the New Testament taught that faith was voluntary, not hereditary. Baptism, in turn, was to be practiced in obedience to the inward transformation that faith wrought in the life of the individual believer. Re-baptizing himself as an adult believer, Smyth, in turn, performed the ritual upon the former Anglicans who comprised his flock, in the process establishing the first Baptist congregation in the world. While believer's baptism became the theological hallmark of the Baptist faith and the sacramental dividing point from most other Protestants, Smyth also rejected worship liturgy in favor of spontaneity and established pastors and deacons as the twofold offices within the local church.

Despite Smyth's contribution as co-founder of the Baptist faith, in 1611 the former Anglican continued his personal spiritual quest and began to embrace Mennonite doctrines. A subgroup of sixteenth-century radical dissenters known as Anabaptists, Mennonites shared the Baptist aversion to infant baptism and church hierarchy. As pacifists, Mennonites also rejected participation in government and the taking of oaths, positions dissimilar from Baptists.

Absent Smyth and some lay persons who followed his migration out of Baptist life, Helwys assumed leadership of the group. That same year, in collaboration with about a dozen church members, he authored what is considered to be the first Baptist statement of faith, *A Declaration of Faith of English People Remaining at Amsterdam in Holland*. Whereas creeds—opposed by Baptists—served as formal doctrinal statements to which church members were obligated to subscribe, Helwys's *Declaration* was a confession, that is, a non-binding statement of beliefs understood to represent a general consensus of those issuing the statement. Thus began Baptists' historical journey as a "confessional" people who clung to the New Testament text as their final written authority, rather than to human-constructed doctrinal formulas.

Insisting upon believer's baptism, and rejecting creeds, church hierarchy, and human authorities, Helwys and his little band of Baptists stood as David before Goliath in defiance of the English state church. Charged as heretics, these earliest Baptists held to basic Christian orthodoxy and insisted that the church's tradition of infant baptism corrupted biblical teachings. As to ecclesiastical matters, they embraced congregationalism, championed the autonomy of the local church, and advocated the office of pastor rather than priest as the New Testament model.

Evidencing boldness in both pen and action, Helwys led his flock back to England and into the jurisdiction of their persecutors. Perhaps if they had stopped at this point, the Baptist story might have unfolded differently. But in 1612, Helwys, now in England and pastoring his flock in Spitalfield in East London, distributed another writing, *A Short Declaration of the Mystery of Iniquity*. Whereas his *Declaration of Faith* served as a theological apologetic, *Mystery of Iniquity* boldly took an ax to the political, legal, and ecclesiastical framework of England and the authority of the Roman Catholic Church at large. Papacy and Puritanism alike fell under Helwys's pen as he elaborated upon what is considered to be the first written publication in the English language advocating religious liberty for everyone. To drive the point home, the emboldened Helwys sent a copy of the volume, including a personal note, to King James I (who the previous year had commissioned the printing of the King James Bible). "The King," Helwys declared, "is a mortal man, and not God, therefore he hath no power over the mortal souls of his subjects to make laws and ordinances for them and to set spiritual Lords over them." For his audacity in challenging king and church, Helwys was cast into prison, where he perished, even as the religious principles of freedom he championed refused to die.

In the wake of Helwys's death, Baptists in England remained under a cloud of suspicion and scrutiny from church and state authorities. Meeting quietly in homes and alleys, they defiantly advocated freedom of religion and conscience. New adherents trickled into their fellowship as these early Baptists set about convincing the world of their Christian orthodoxy and the biblical foundation of freedom.

The broader theological landscape undergirding religious liberty and separation of church and state sketched out by both Smyth and Helwys included voluntary faith, believer's baptism, congregational church polity, and the right of the individual to read and interpret scripture. While this last tenet was widely accepted by Protestants under the rubric of the priesthood of all believers, many Christians believed that Baptists advocated too many liberties in terms of voluntary faith. And while congregational church polity found some resonance among dissenters at large, believer's baptism remained an impenetrable barrier between Baptists and most other Christians. This barrier widened when sometime in the 1630s

Baptists rejected pouring and sprinkling, the prevailing modes of baptism, in favor of what they came to consider the biblical method: immersion.

Defending their faith outwardly, early English Baptists also debated their faith internally. Although the earliest Baptists embraced Arminian theology (and eventually became known as General Baptists, for their belief that Christ's death was for all persons), by 1638 a second strain of Baptists emerged: Particular Baptists. These Baptists embraced the theology of Protestant Reformer John Calvin and insisted that Christ's death was only for certain individuals, known as the "elect." These two theologically distinct variations of Baptists represented a larger conversation taking place in Protestant life of the era, and both groups of Baptists traversed periods of growth and decline in the decades and centuries following.

ROGER WILLIAMS AND JOHN CLARKE
CHAMPIONS OF DEMOCRACY AND FREEDOM IN THE COLONIES

A freedom nexus established, orthodoxy defended, biblical immersion "recovered," and theological diversity emerging, the Baptist faith, in turn, migrated to the New World, following in the wake of the Puritans and Separatists. The coming of Baptists to the American colonies began innocently enough when a young lawyer-turned-minister stepped off a ship in Boston in February 1631 following a two-month winter journey on the high seas. Fleeing with his wife to the Massachusetts Bay Colony, Roger Williams (c. 1604-1684), a Separatist, thus avoided almost certain imprisonment in England.

Boston's Puritan leaders welcomed Williams, a former chaplain in the Church of England, with open arms. To their surprise, however, he turned down their offer to pastor the fledgling church in Boston, declaring that he could not pastor a church that had yet to completely separate from the Church of England. As a lawyer, Williams had witnessed the persecution of dissenters, and their mistreatment and punishment as heretics had left the young man distrustful of the Church and suspicious of civil authorities.

Thus began an uneasy five-year period in which Williams spent time as an itinerant preacher in Boston and pastor in Salem while his religious views grew increasingly radical. His harsh criticisms of the Church of England, insistence on religious freedom for all citizens, and denial that government had spiritual authority over citizens led colonial leaders to label his views as the work of Satan. Banished from the Massachusetts colony in late 1635, Williams fled into the wilderness, where in the midst of a brutal New England winter he became a homeless outcast, sleeping in hollow logs in the dark forest and living off roots and berries. He may have agonized over the circumstances that led to his wilderness exile, but there are no indications that he regretted his religious convictions.

Just when it seemed Williams's life would end in an untimely death in the wilderness, his relationship with the region's Indians proved to be his salvation. A visionary man with few equals in his day, Williams was one of the earliest and most vocal advocates for Indian rights. Having befriended the natives living in and around Massachusetts, his relationship with them paid off when they found him and offered him shelter until spring arrived.

With the coming of summer, a grateful Williams, now leading a small band of nomadic Separatists and other dissenters who had searched him out following the spring thaw, purchased land from the Indians and founded a settlement, aptly named Providence. Other settlements followed in the next few years, and in 1644, English authorities granted a colonial charter, formally establishing Rhode Island as the most revolutionary and forward-looking colony in the New World. A model for what would one day become a new nation, the Rhode Island Colony from its inception was a land in which government and church remained separate (Williams coined the term "wall of separation" to describe the Baptist and American position regarding church and state relations), pluralism was welcomed, full religious liberty was granted to all citizens, and governance was administrated in the form of a secular democracy. While the rest of the world (including the theocracies of colonial New England) clung to church-state regimes, Williams became the father of modern democracy, laying the foundation of modern governance some 140 years before the establishment of the American nation.

While the world remembers Williams as the founder of modern democracy, the former Anglican chaplain accomplished another notable achievement: founding the earliest Baptist church in America. In 1639, three years after establishing Providence, Williams, having embraced the Baptist faith, founded in his settlement the first Baptist church in the New World. Still existing in present-day Providence, Rhode Island, the church is known as the First Baptist Church of America. To future Baptists in America, the courageous and energetic Williams thus bequeathed the freedom principles that first sprouted in Amsterdam and found full expression among English Baptists before finding even more fertile ground in the American colonies. He most clearly articulated his views on complete religious liberty in *The Bloudy Tenet of Persecution* (1644) and *The Bloudy Tenet Yet More Bloudy* (1652), two volumes that chronicled religious persecution and defined the Baptist mission and purpose in colonial America.

Although Williams remained faithful to Baptist freedoms and ideals, his formal Baptist sojourn came to a quick end, as his pilgrimage led him to other spiritual pastures as a Seeker. Upon Williams's foundation soon stepped John Clarke (1609-1676), co-founder of the Rhode Island Colony, medical doctor, and Baptist minister. About the same time that Williams established a Baptist church in Providence, Clarke helped found the city of Newport; by 1644, he established a Baptist congregation in the town, now recognized as the second oldest Baptist church in America. In the decades following, Clarke became one of the leading Baptist figures in the entire colonies, although at that time public recognition as a Baptist outside of Rhode Island was personally dangerous.

The story of Baptists in colonial America from 1639 through the end of the century was one of survival and perseverance, in which John Clarke's footsteps tread heavily. From the refuge of Rhode Island, the Baptist faith spread into Massachusetts, where the faithful few endured beatings, whippings, jailings, and other persecutions. One of the persecuted, an elderly gentlemen by the name of William Witter (c. 1584-1659), first ran afoul of Massachusetts law in 1643 and was summoned before the Salem court the following year for declaring infant baptism a sin. Signaling the contempt with which Baptists were held, the Massachusetts Bay Colony in 1644 passed a law banishing individuals who denied infant baptism; many more anti-Baptist laws were passed in the years immediately following. Witter remained under a cloud of suspicion by authorities in the years following, and in 1651, the then-blind man appealed to John Clarke to come to his house and conduct a worship service, a clearly illegal activity in the colony.

Despite the danger at hand, Clarke and two other Newport members, John Crandall (1612-1676) and Obadiah Holmes (1606-1682), responded to Witter's request. Holmes, a former resident of the Massachusetts colony, had recently moved to Newport to escape religious persecution. While visiting with Witter at his home in Lynn in July 1651, the Newport trio were arrested and jailed for conducting an illegal worship service. Clarke protested the fines levied upon the three, to which Massachusetts Governor John Endecott retorted that Clarke deserved death and should be executed by hanging. Nonetheless, the fines for Clarke and Crandall were paid, although Holmes refused an offer to pay his fine. Instead, the former Massachusetts citizen endured thirty lashes. At the time of his whipping and in the presence of a gathered crowd, Holmes proclaimed himself joyful and cheerful and insisted that his lashing felt like roses striking his back. Returning to Newport in 1652 following his incarceration, the scarred but yet-defiant Holmes succeeded Clarke as pastor of the Newport congregation.

The 1651 arrest and Holmes's whipping led Clarke the following year to compose a volume, *Ill Newes from New England, or a Narrative of New England's Persecutions*, launching the former pastor's religious freedom crusade in the colonies and a career in Rhode Island politics. Working alongside Williams, Clarke traveled to England and persuaded King Charles II in 1663 to grant a new royal charter formalizing religious freedom in Rhode Island. Supporting his travels and ministry through his medical practice, Clarke also served as deputy governor of Rhode Island from 1669 to 1672, and upon his death in 1676, his will established the first educational trust fund in the United States.

In the broader perspective, Clarke's *Ill Newes* signaled that many Baptists in the New World, anchored in Rhode Island, would not relent until religious liberty and separation of church and state replaced colonial theocracies. At the same time, Puritan civil authorities at large were determined to prevent Baptists (and Quakers, who shared Baptists' freedom convictions) from moving into their jurisdictions. In the decades following, the battle between freedom and theocracy further defined the Baptist identity in America. When Massachusetts in 1654 enacted laws to tax citizens in order to fund the Congregational Church, Baptists refused to pay; in so doing, they faced whipping, prison, branding, loss of physical extremities, and other cruel punishments. Yet, the 1662 English Act of Uniformity led to an increase in dissenters migrating to the colonies, despite the threats of persecution. As a result, Baptist congregations were founded near Swansea (1663) and in Boston (1665).

Constantly persecuted, their pastors in and out of jail, and laws preventing the use of buildings for worship, Baptists in Massachusetts struggled for their survival, with few Baptist congregations existing in the colony at the dawn of the eighteenth century. Meanwhile, a Baptist congregation was established in 1682 in Kittery, Maine, but in 1696, the congregation migrated to Charleston, South Carolina, seeking friendly climes, and in the process established the first Baptist church in the South. By 1704, another Baptist congregation had been established at Groton, Connecticut.

> In the broader perspective, Clarke's *Ill Newes* signaled that many Baptists in the New World, anchored in Rhode Island, would not relent until religious liberty and separation of church and state replaced colonial theocracies.

In short, Puritan authorities in the New England colonies largely kept Baptists at bay throughout the seventeenth century, confining them primarily to Rhode Island. The hostility in New England led some Baptists to migrate to the Middle Colonies, a relative haven of religious tolerance, thanks to William

Penn and the Quakers. Baptists established congregations in Pennsylvania and New Jersey during the last two decades of the century, and the leading Baptist figure of the region was Elias Keach, pastor of the church in Pennepek, Pennsylvania. A successful church starter and espousing moderate theology, Keach avoided internal controversies that were distracting some Baptist congregations, including escalating debates over the doctrine of predestination, questions over the appropriateness of music in worship, and disagreements over whether worship should be conducted on the Sabbath rather than Sunday.

Thus, by the turn of the eighteenth century, the contours of Baptist life in colonial America were set. Outwardly united in advocating freedom of religion in the New World and internally committed to voluntary faith, Baptists struggled to survive the pressures of persecutions at the hands of colonial theocracies and sought to address mounting internal divisions over matters of theology and ecclesiology.

ENGLISH BAPTISTS
TRIALS FROM WITHIN

Meanwhile back in England, Baptists seemed to be on firmer footing. During their first few decades, the enterprising sect used public debates and technology—the printing press—to spread their message of freedom. So successful was the marketing campaign that their opponents at times felt overwhelmed by the Baptist media blitz; and by the 1650s, Baptists had gained enough traction in the public marketplace of ideas that congregations began joining together to issue formal statements of belief.

Committed to freedom of conscience, English Baptists rejected the paradigm of creeds that had prescribed and enforced Christian doctrine since the days of the early church. Putting their faith to paper in the form of non-authoritative confessions, while acknowledging the Bible as their only trustworthy guide, they forged a new theological path. While General Baptist and Particular

Baptist confessions focused on Arminian and Calvinistic theology, respectively, both groups affirmed believer's baptism, the authority of scripture, and religious liberty. Inherent within the theology of both groups resided a tension that remains to this day: a compulsion within the community to voice acceptable doctrinal beliefs within the broader context of respecting and preserving the freedom of individual conscience.

The dissenters, in short, understood that although community necessitated structure and order, voluntary faith was impossible apart from freedom. Local church autonomy, in turn, provided the vessel for preserving both responsibility and freedom. Should Baptist individuals feel too constrained by their local congregation, they did not have to forsake the Baptist faith, but instead were free to associate with a more suitable Baptist congregation.

In addition to the General and Particular divisions over theology, differences among local seventeenth-century English Baptist congregations varied greatly over such issues as ministerial ordination (necessary or not) and church offices (some congregations accepted women deacons and allowed women to preach). Communion and worship served as two of the more contentious issues. Local printers were probably pleased when a decade-long war of printed words erupted between William Kiffin (1616-1701), wealthy merchant-minister and leading Baptist of his day and a staunch advocate of closed communion (available only to properly baptized persons), and John Bunyan (1628-1688), of *Pilgrim's Progress* fame and advocator of open communion (accessible to any true Christian). From 1672 to 1681, the two men squared off in a publishing duel that their fellow Baptists of the era followed closely. Kiffin's view prevailed in the short term, as Bunyan's progressive view proved ahead of his time.

While the communion debate took place at a theological level, the worship wars of the seventeenth century evoked widespread emotion and passion. Worship services of the era were spontaneous, with no formal prayers or structured order of service, although a sermon or two, prayers here and there, responses from lay persons, and a collection of money for the poor would typically take place at some point during the worship time. Although foot washing was a controversial practice in some cases, the locus of seventeenth-century worship wars was music. For decades, Baptists resisted both instrumentation and singing in general, but in the closing decades of the 1600s, again to the delight of printers, a handful of progressive Baptists, the most famous of whom was the minister and songwriter Benjamin Keach (1640-1704), composer of hundreds of hymns, vied with anti-music advocates in a battle of pamphlets and tracts. Baptists in local congregations throughout England for several decades argued over the propriety of singing in church, with pro-music views eventually winning the argument among first Particular and then General Baptists by the mid-eighteenth century.

The passage of the Toleration Act of 1689 led to a greater focus on internal church matters. This government decree created public maneuvering room for dissenters but stopped short of allowing full religious liberty. Granted state permission to exist and spread their faith, English Baptists now enjoyed opportunities foreign to their fellow believers in the American colonies. And yet, the story of much of eighteenth-century English Baptist life proved less inspiring than it did disturbing, as the General and Particular divisions became battle lines in a contest for the theological loyalty of English Baptists.

Historians yet debate the exact reasons behind the Baptist doctrinal boxing match that erupted in the eighteenth century. However, the fact is undisputed that in the larger context of the era, human reasoning, aided by advances in scientific and philosophical thought, challenged the prism of theology through which truth was commonly viewed. Many General Baptists of the century melded their doctrine with Enlightenment principles, producing a theology that downplayed the historical conceptualization of the Trinity and the full humanity and full deity of Christ. Doctrinally disengaged, many churches found themselves arguing over legalities (such as the proper way to sing in church, the appropriateness of secular entertainment, and marriage outside of the faith) that seemed oddly out of place for theological liberals.

At the same time, Particular Baptists wandered off in the opposite direction, growing increasingly strident and strict in their Calvinistic pursuits. Turning to Presbyterian theologians (rather than Enlightenment thinkers) to buttress their theology, many embraced a doctrine of God's complete sovereignty that disavowed any human responsibility for preaching the gospel to sinners and relieved believers from the burden of living as saints. John Gill (1696-1771), pastor of the Horsleydown Strict Baptist Church for over fifty years, became the recognized figurehead of this Calvinistic Baptist expression of Christianity in which theologically conservative believers lost interest in evangelism and a lived faith.

Fortunately, toward the end of the century, both groups of English Baptists were rescued from their wayward excesses. General Baptists reclaimed orthodoxy and evangelism thanks to the tireless efforts of a Baptist convert and minister, Dan Taylor (1738-1816). Taylor's "New Connection" of churches infused into General Baptist life of the late 1700s the excitement of "Experimental Religion" that he borrowed from the Methodists, a denomination birthed from the early-eighteenth-century revival ministries of John and Charles Wesley. At the same time, the Calvinistic Particular Baptists found their lofty theology increasingly pricked by a generation of ministers in the Northamptonshire Association who had been influenced by the Wesleyan emphasis on personal piety and social ministry. When, in 1779, Robert Hall, Sr. (1728-1791), pastor of a congregation in Leicester, preached a sermon during the annual association meeting in which he declared his intent to remove from Baptist life the "stumbling-block" of Calvinism, the die was cast: something new was afoot, and it would be greater than anyone at that time could have imagined.

Leaving the English Baptists, who were emerging from the doldrums of theologies gone astray from their roots and poised to step upon the threshold of an entirely new chapter in Baptist life, the story now returns to Baptists in America and their coming of age.

ISAAC BACKUS AND JOHN LELAND
SHAPERS OF THE AMERICAN NATION

The founding of America as the world's first secular nation—a pluralistic nation with a distinctly Christian influence, yet founded upon the core Baptist principles of religious liberty and separation of church and state—owes much to the tireless efforts of Isaac Backus and John Leland. Prior to their arrival, however, Baptists experienced significant transformation, much of it not of their own making.

With only twenty-four congregations and less than 900 adherents at the turn of the eighteenth century, Baptists remained somewhat of an oddity in colonial America. Few Americans of that day would have personally known a Baptist, much less had an inkling that the tiny religious sect would provide the key ideological underpinnings of a nation not yet formed. From the safety of democratic Rhode Island, these little-known Baptists slowly ventured forth into the hostile theocracies of New England and beyond. Initially, they braved waves of persecution from state churches that devoted themselves to silencing anyone who disobeyed or questioned their divine mandate to dispense the law and rule over culture and society; and in some instances by clumsy and yet friendly efforts, the establishment tried to convert Baptists to the Congregational faith.

The greatest Baptist advance of the first half of the century, however, took place in the Middle Colonies, a refuge of religious toleration wedged between the Congregational theocracies in the North and Anglican theocracies in the South. While a handful of Baptist congregations sprung up in Delaware and New Jersey, Pennsylvania afforded greater opportunity for Baptists to take root. The first permanent Baptist association in America, the Philadelphia Association, was formed in Pennsylvania in 1707. This influential body in 1742 adopted a confession of faith that affirmed the centrality of the local church, defined the association as assisting local churches, and established the limited powers and authority of the association, in the process shaping the historical role of associations in Baptist life.

In 1763, the Philadelphia Association sent Baptist minister and Princeton graduate James Manning (1738-1791) to Rhode Island to establish a Baptist college. From the efforts of Manning and the association, Rhode Island College in 1764 was chartered in Warren, Rhode Island, the third-oldest college in New England, and the first Baptist school of higher education. While presiding over the college, Manning also pastored First Baptist Church in Providence from 1771 to 1791. During this time, he advocated for religious liberty and served as a Rhode Island congressional delegate following the American Revolution.

The founding of America as the world's first secular nation—a pluralistic nation with a distinctly Christian influence, yet founded upon the core Baptist principles of religious liberty and separation of church and state—owes much to the tireless efforts of Isaac Backus and John Leland.

While the Middle Colonies and Rhode Island remained exceptions to the rule of persecution for religious dissenters, establishment churches confronted problems of their own. Addressing the challenges posed by Baptists would have been a much easier task for the colonial theocracies if not for a growing internal dilemma: the state-supported Congregational Church of the Upper Colonies began losing members and, in turn, influence as succeeding generations of Puritans became less fervent in their faith. Desperate to maintain authority over culture and society, Congregationalists in the second half of the seventeenth century loosened the definition of church membership in an attempt to bolster membership levels. By the dawn of the eighteenth century, many church members, although baptized as infants, were merely names on membership rolls.

The expanding American frontier further compounded establishment church problems: frontier colonists frequently had a different social status and political persuasion than Congregational congregations in the larger, urban coastal cities. While Congregationalists struggled on the frontier, Baptists experienced less persecution in colonial outposts.

Even so, Baptists remained few, isolated, and largely unknown until something entirely new swept through the colonies: religious revival. Although Jonathan Edwards (1703-1758), Congregationalist pastor and Calvinist theologian in Northampton, Massachusetts, is remembered as the foremost figure of the Great Awakening, the revival that his church experienced was short-lived and had no discernible lasting effects on church attendance. To other preachers and evangelists, including Congregationalist evangelists in

America and the Wesleys and George Whitefield from England, goes the bulk of the credit for fanning the flames of widespread revival in the New England colonies. Preaching the fury of God, describing in detail the eternal fires and torments of hell, and insisting that salvation was equally available to anyone who voiced belief in God, revival preachers offered personal certainty and eternal security at a time in history when scientific discoveries and theories, posing unprecedented challenges to a God-centric worldview, created increasing discomfort in the Calvinist-laden colonies.

While the emotional fervor of the Great Awakening found expression primarily in the 1730s and 1740s, the longer-term influence of the revivals led to a remarkable theological shift upon the colonial landscape. Making personal professions of faith, revival converts seized from traditional Congregationalism ownership of the salvation process. Now residing in the hearts of men and women rather than in the act of infant baptism and on the rolls of state churches, salvation became both mobile and personal. Former Congregationalists by the thousands left the state churches, with as many as half of all Congregationalists finding a new home in Baptist life, drawn by the experiential nature of the Baptist faith and identifying with the Baptist emphasis on a regenerate church membership as expressed in believer's baptism.

Meanwhile, Baptists, although contributing no significant leadership to the Great Awakening, had responded to the revivals by informally dividing into two camps: Regular Baptists, who were largely urban and suspicious of the emotional-saturated revivals, and Separate Baptists, who tended to be rural in nature and expressed openness to revival fervor. The spiritual heritage of Regular Baptists remains to this day in many city congregations with relatively formal worship services, while Separate Baptists of the late eighteenth century found receptivity on the southern frontier, expressed in an evangelical intensity and warmness still prevalent throughout much of the modern South.

From Congregationalist ranks in the 1750s stepped individuals who became outstanding leaders in Baptist life. Shubal Stearns (1706-1771), Daniel Marshall (1706-1784), and Martha Stearns Marshall (1700s), all from New England, converted to the Separate Baptist faith in the early 1750s and migrated to the rural community of Sandy Creek, North Carolina, where they quickly became the most popular preachers on the southern frontier. Their emotional evangelistic methodology and Arminian-influenced theology resulted in an explosion of Baptist congregations in North Carolina and beyond over the next few decades. According to some accounts, Martha was the best preacher of the lot.

Also from a Congregational background, Isaac Backus (1724-1806) of Connecticut became a Baptist in 1751 and quickly emerged as the new leading spokesperson for Baptists in the North on the subject of religious freedom. Theocratic Massachusetts since the late seventeenth century had forced Baptists and other dissenters to pay taxes to fund the state Congregational Church, confiscating personal property when met with refusal. The newly-converted Backus soon faced the ire of the establishment church. In fact, the Massachusetts colony imprisoned his elderly and ailing mother, Elizabeth, in 1752, in response to her forsaking Congregationalism and refusing to pay back taxes to the church. Although the incident caused a public outcry that led to a speedy release, son Isaac spent the remainder of his life as a public and vocal proponent of religious liberty and opponent of the entanglement of church and state.

Elizabeth's imprisonment proved to be a precursor of things to come, as persecution of Baptists from the 1750s through the American Revolution reached new heights. In New England, and especially in Massachusetts, Baptists came under greater pressure to abandon their dissenting views and voluntarily support the state church.

However, the full wrath of theocratic fury fell upon Virginia Baptists. Prior to 1750, the establishment church in the Virginia colony, the Anglican (Episcopal) Church, managed to keep religious opposition to a minimum. While the few dissenters living on the Virginia frontier co-existed uneasily with the Anglican Church—after all, what harm could they do on the outposts of civilization—dissent was otherwise kept in check by constant threats of whippings and fines.

Thanks to the revivals, however, Baptists began arriving in Virginia in force by the late 1750s. Not content to remain solely within the frontier communities, and insisting on their right to proselytize, the Baptist immigrants found receptivity among the common people, while their public expressions of faith angered government and Anglican Church officials. In response, church and state leaders in Virginia, already feeling pressure from growing revolutionary sentiment, for the next two decades enacted a campaign to beat Baptists into submission.

The persecutions endured by Virginia Baptists from the early 1760s through the late 1770s were horrible and often bloody. Denying Baptists basic freedoms, preachers were beaten, whipped, mobbed, stoned, and urinated upon while in the pulpit. In addition, some were shot, dynamited, and tortured by near-drowning. Laity faced the prospect of the seizure of property for not paying religious taxes. Church buildings were shuttered and meetings violently broken up. In short, "Christian" government officials terrorized Baptists in a desperate effort to preserve their theocracies at the very time their citizenry at large were agitating for freedom from England.

Denied freedom of religion and victimized by domestic terrorism, many Baptists in Virginia became ardent supporters of revolution against England, committing themselves to securing religious liberty for all and separation of church and state in the new nation. Baptist support for the war effort, in turn, pressured Virginia officials to forsake persecuting the Baptists in exchange for their alliance against England. Many Baptists fought valiantly as revolutionary soldiers. And as the new nation took shape in the years immediately following the Declaration of Independence, Baptists in Virginia worked with James Madison and Thomas Jefferson in writing (1779) and enacting (1786) the Virginia Statute of Religious Freedom. Less than a decade removed from harsh persecution, Baptists in Virginia finally breathed sighs of relief.

Religious liberty and separation of church and state secured in Virginia, Baptists of that state turned their attention to the American nation. John Leland (1754-1841), formerly of Massachusetts prior to moving to Virginia, by 1786 stood as the recognized spokesperson of Baptists in Virginia. One of the most successful Baptist evangelists of his era, Leland was also politically savvy and influential, leading Baptist support for the Virginia Statute for Religious Freedom. Afterward, Leland's influence with Madison and Jefferson over the next five years helped secure religious freedom in the new United States of America, a secular nation that separated church from state and granted religious liberty to all in the First Amendment to the Constitution (1791).

To be sure, the attainment of religious freedom, the crowning achievement of Baptists in America of the seventeenth and eighteenth centuries, could not be attributed to one person. While Leland served as the most visible Baptist in Virginia who assisted in securing First Amendment religious liberties, and Isaac Backus the most notable in New England, Baptist common folk throughout the newly-formed nation also supported the effort. In all the theocratic colonies, Baptists, lay and clergy alike, lifted their voices, risked their lives, and cast their votes in support of religious freedom during the formative years of the new nation. They, in turn, stood upon the shoulders of their Baptist forebears whose blood and beatings paved the way for freedom.

Beginning with John Smyth, Thomas Helwys, Roger Williams, and John Clarke, generations of Baptist freedom fighters on both sides of the Atlantic poured their lives into the crucible from which was forged the religious freedoms secured within the First Amendment to the United States Constitution. The great battle had been won, the identity of Baptists forever sealed. Church and state now separated for the first time in history, Baptists in America set about spreading their faith, while Baptists in England, enjoying a degree of religious toleration and harnessing internal diversions, reexamined the fate of people living in distant lands.

TWO

MISSIONARIES AND EVANGELISTS

1792-1844

William Carey (1761-1834), the unlikeliest of heroes, stumbled into the vacuum created in Baptist life by the ascendancy of Calvinism. Taken to its logical conclusion, Calvinism was an approach to religion in which faith and action were inconsequential because everything had been predetermined prior to creation.

Although now less acrimonious and again experiencing growth, British Baptists in the 1780s could not possibly have foreseen that a poor, balding, journeymen shoemaker, Carey, would soon become the most important figure in English Baptist life since Smyth and Helwys. Nor could anyone have guessed that Carey's life would have global impact far beyond his years on earth.

One unremarkable day near the end of the summer of 1785, a Particular Baptist congregation in Olney, after enduring a summer of Carey's painfully poor sermons, refused to ordain the young man. Disillusioned but determined, the shoemaker refused to quit. Baptized only two years prior by John Ryland, Jr. (1753-1825), who was unimpressed with the new convert, Carey was used to people looking down on him. So in the wake of his rejection by the Olney church, he turned to the two things he knew he could do well: repairing shoes and learning new languages. Finding security in shoes and books, Carey doggedly continued his pursuit of ordination; and in 1786, the congregation in Olney reluctantly ordained the shoemaker and sent him on his way, relieved to be rid of him.

Carey's troubles continued. In 1787, now pastoring the church in Moulton while repairing shoes and teaching geography to a handful of students, the father of the man who had baptized Carey publicly humiliated him. The occasion was a meeting of the ministers of the Northamptonshire Association. During the meeting, Carey wondered aloud whether Christ's command in Matthew 28 to preach the gospel to the ends of the world applied to the present day, after which John Ryland, Sr. (1723-1792) demanded that Carey sit down and shut up, insisting that if God wanted to convert the heathen, God would do so without the help of missionaries. Calvinism, it seemed, had not yet loosened its claustrophobic grip upon Particular Baptists.

Carey's thoughts on his way home after his verbal lashing are not known, but the undaunted young man again turned to books. This time he began writing a volume, privately penning his growing obsession with the concept of doing missionary work among the "heathen" living in foreign lands.

Five years after being told to sit down and shut up, Carey, in May 1792, was given a chance to speak at the Nottingham Association. The publication of his missionary volume, *An Enquiry into the Obligations of Christians to use*

Means for the Conversion of the Heathens, had preceded this speaking engagement. Preaching from Isaiah 54:2, Carey called upon his fellow pastors to "expect great things from God" and "attempt great things for God." When his listeners seemed unmoved following the sermon, he prompted associational director Andrew Fuller (1754-1815) to call for discussion. In 1785, Fuller had published a book (*The Gospel Worthy of All Acceptance*) declaring that the gospel should be preached to all persons, not merely the elect, thus challenging normative Calvinism.

The ensuing dialogue eventually led to the formation in October 1792 of the Particular Baptist Society for Propagating the Gospel among the Heathen (later renamed Baptist Missionary Society). Carey, Fuller, and Ryland, Jr., serving among the charter members, set about to raise funding. The following year, Carey and his family departed for India, his missionary fervor and language skills overshadowing the misgivings of his wife Dorothy. Thus, the modern missionary movement began, thanks to the unflagging determination of a poor, awkward preacher who repeatedly refused to take "no" for an answer.

In a larger perspective, the fulfillment of William Carey's vision in 1792 redirected Baptist energy and served as a catalyst in many areas of Baptist life. Missions energy and vision paved the way for the formation of national Baptist denominational organizations, initiated a debate on how best to do missions, created controversy at the local church level, provided a catalyst for educational efforts among Baptists, highlighted racial tensions in America, tilted the theological discourse toward Arminianism, and accompanied a new era of evangelical emphasis.

In Britain, an array of Baptist organizations sprouted out from the hub of missions in the early decades of the century. The independent Baptist Missionary Society, under the leadership of Fuller, expanded and grew; and in 1813, Particular Baptists formed the Baptist Union with a primary focus on missions and secondary emphases on Christian education, Sunday Schools, evangelism, and the construction of church buildings. Remaining in the shadow of the Baptist Missionary Society for most of the century, the Baptist Union nonetheless slowly generated more denominational cohesion among independent-minded Particular Baptists.

Across the theological aisle, the New Connection of General Baptists formed their own Foreign General Baptist Mission board in 1816 and began work in India. At the same time, the Baptist Society for the Encouragement and Support of Itinerant Preaching, formed in 1797, worked with Baptist colleges in Britain in sending out students on home mission projects, eventually evolving into the Home Mission Society.

Ascendant educational endeavors paralleled a growing missionary emphasis. While Bristol Baptist College (the first Baptist institution of higher education), had been established in 1679, not until the early nineteenth century did British Baptists enter their golden era of higher education. In 1810, Regent's Park College (as it came to be known) was founded, soon becoming British Baptists' leading educational institution. At the same time, growing interest in missions among students magnified the place of higher education in British Baptist life. In short, Baptist life in Britain during the early nineteenth century became more mission-minded, denominationally-centric, and educationally equipped.

Meanwhile, religious life in America experienced widespread transformation through the Second Great Awakening. Beginning early in the century and lasting into the 1840s, revival fires spread throughout the nation. In the North, the religious fervor resulted in the formation of the American Bible Society (1816), the temperance movement, abolitionist organizations, and new faith groups (including the Church of Jesus Christ of Latter Day Saints, or Mormons). Revival in the southern states took the form of emotion-laden rural camp meetings that focused on personal salvation and morality, denounced sins such as card playing and dancing, and further eroded Calvinistic tenets. For Baptists in the South, the revivals attracted new converts to frontier congregations and witnessed an exodus of others, particularly in the formation of the Church of Christ.

While English Baptists gradually coalesced around various mission-minded denominational structures, Carey's missionary vision found especially fertile soil in revivalist-stoked America. Freed from the constraints of religious persecution and disentangling themselves from strict Calvinism, Baptists in America became captivated by Carey's exploits, further fanning evangelistic embers. Massachusetts Baptists formed a missionary society in 1803, followed by New York Baptists in 1807. Congregationalists, however, played a critical role in spurring Baptists to action on a national scale.

On a summer Saturday afternoon in 1806, a group of Congregationalist students attending Williams College in Massachusetts, found themselves out in the open in a sudden thunderstorm and ducked under hay sheaves for shelter. The storm interrupted their prayer session for missions, one of many such prayer meetings they had conducted. Yet, this time turned out to be different, for as the students huddled under the hay that soggy day, they resolved to become involved in foreign missionary work.

The "Brethren," as they were known, graduated from college and most went on to newly-formed Andover Seminary, where they met Adoniram Judson (1788-1850), a graduate of Brown University who had recently dedicated his life to mission service. Judson and fellow student Samuel Mills (1783-1818), in turn, influenced Congregationalists to form the American Board of Commissioners for Foreign Missions in 1810. The first such national organization in America, the board appointed Adoniram and Ann Judson to serve as missionaries in India and convinced Mills to remain in the states in a support role. Another of the brethren, Luther Rice (1783-1836), was also soon appointed as a missionary to India.

En route to India, Judson, while studying baptism in the Greek New Testament, concluded that immersion was the proper mode. Upon their arrival in Calcutta, the Judsons were baptized as Baptists, and Rice soon thereafter. Resigning from the Congregational mission board, the Judsons assumed ministry as Baptists, while Rice, single, returned to the states to raise funds for the mission work.

Speaking to Baptist congregations, associations, and the handful of local and regional missionary associations already in existence, Rice worked tirelessly, helping form new local and regional mission societies. He eventually envisioned drawing together the growing number of local and regional bodies into one nationwide organization, similar to that of the Congregationalists. Rice's vision came to pass in 1814 with the formation of the General Missionary Convention of the Baptist Denomination in the United States of America for Foreign Missions (or Triennial Convention), the first national Baptist mission organization in America.

Headquartered in Philadelphia and supported by the Philadelphia Baptist Association, the convention provided a way for Baptists in America to finance the work of the Judsons and other foreign missionaries and opened the door for involvement in other denominational endeavors. Advocating for public schools, publication of Bibles, and Christian higher education, the convention also opposed the United States Indian Removal Act of 1830 and founded the American Baptist Home Mission Society in 1832, the latter for work among Indians and the American frontier at large.

Not all Baptists in America, however, supported mission work and other denominational endeavors. Strict Calvinistic theology, while fading, remained influential enough to effect an anti-missions movement that in the 1820s and 1830s led to widespread divisions within associations and among local congregations. Anti-mission forces, who became known as Primitive Baptists, insisted that the mission movement was without biblical precedent and subverted local church authority. Especially strong in the rural South, representatives, meeting at Black Rock, Maryland, in 1832, formalized the larger ideology of the movement. Condemning the trend away from Calvinism that began with Andrew Fuller, the Black Rock Document rejected, in addition to mission boards, Sunday Schools, Bible societies, tract societies, theological schools, and protracted revival meetings. In short, Primitive Baptists denied the validity of all Christian organizations except the local congregation, and they retained a strong presence in Baptist life through the nineteenth century.

Nonetheless, the mission movement catalyzed denominationalism to such an extent that Baptists in America as a whole also experienced a transformation in the parallel realm of education. While an anti-intellectual climate characterized much of Baptist life on the American frontier at the turn of the nineteenth century, the challenges of taking the gospel to other nations and the pastoral demands of growing city congregations necessitated formal training. Newton Theological Institution, established in Newton Centre, Massachusetts, in 1826 with the support of the Triennial Convention, became Baptists' first seminary in America. Numerous Baptist institutions of higher education sprang up to assist Baptist work in the South, including Mississippi College (1826), Furman University in South Carolina (1826), the University of Richmond in Virginia (1830), Mercer University in Georgia (1833), and Wake Forest in North Carolina (1834).

Even as Baptists embraced missions, national denominationalism, and ministerial education, however, the early nineteenth century witnessed internal struggles over the issue of slavery, which forced a reexamination of Baptist principles of freedom. William Carey and a handful of other British Baptists preached and spoke against slavery at the turn of the century, while still others remained either neutral or became apologists for slavery. Sam Sharpe, a slave and Baptist laymen in Jamaica who spread the gospel among fellow slaves, led a peaceful but unsuccessful slave uprising, known as the "Baptist War," against plantation owners in 1831; he was killed in defense of freedom. Meanwhile, Free Will Baptists (who had arisen in the eighteenth century in opposition to predestination beliefs espoused by Calvinists) in the North took an initial lead among Baptists in America in advocating freedom for slaves. Yet, for larger Baptist bodies in the United States, slavery proved to be a challenge like no other.

> Even as Baptists embraced missions, national denominationalism, and ministerial education, however, the early nineteenth century witnessed internal struggles over the issue of slavery, which forced a reexamination of Baptist principles of freedom.

John Leland, leading Baptist champion of religious freedom, exemplified the complexity surrounding the growing slavery debate on American soil. Leland advocated freedom for slaves in the 1790s; but in the 1830s, he separated bodily freedom from religious freedom and insisted that slavery was a state issue rather than a religious (or church) issue, scolded abolitionists, and declared that emancipation would disrupt societal structures. During this time frame, American Baptists at large transitioned from a relatively uneasy, if ambivalent, attitude toward slavery to strong abolitionist views in the North and unyielding pro-slavery views in the South. Baptists in the North and South argued from scripture, with a literal biblical apologetic undergirding southern slavery and a broader, contextual interpretation of scripture empowering abolitionists.

While the Nat Turner slave rebellion in Virginia in 1831 and Britain's 1833 Abolition of Slavery Act emboldened northern abolitionists and hardened southern slavery sentiment at large, those events also strained relations among Baptists in particular. Although initially attempting to maintain harmony between northern and southern Baptists, the Triennial Convention, a northern-based body comprised largely of northern Baptists, eventually enacted a policy of neutrality toward slavery. Some northern Baptists responded by withdrawing from the convention and forming abolitionist societies, while Baptists in the South by 1837 began discussing the possibility of forming a southern organization of Baptists. By the early 1840s, many observers recognized that the Triennial Convention would be unable to contain the growing sectional tensions.

Meanwhile, as African American Baptists gradually gained freedoms in the North, slaves increasingly found a home in Baptist life in the South, a result partly of the revivalist fervor of the Baptist faith (resonating with the emotionally-charged nature of African religions) and the numerical growth and newfound prosperity of some white Baptists (their wealth often residing in slave ownership). Echoing Leland's compartmentalization of religious and bodily freedom, white Baptists in the South welcomed African American slaves into their congregations as spiritual equals, while defending black enslavement on the grounds of popular sentiment that blacks were an inferior race.

Affirmation of the religious freedom of slaves resulted in some African Americans becoming distinguished preachers, evangelists, and missionaries. Slave Lott Carey (1780-1828) was converted to Christianity and joined First Baptist Church, Richmond, Virginia, in 1807. Six years later, Carey purchased his freedom, and in 1821, he became the first African American missionary sent to Africa. Numerous others, unable to obtain freedom, preached to and taught slave members of white-controlled congregations. In some cases, slaves were allowed to form their own independent congregations.

Collectively, national revivalist fervor, the missions movement, denominational coalescing, educational advancement, and the growing slavery controversy served as a centrifuge for Baptists in America. From prior relative harmony at the end of the eighteenth century, Baptists by 1844 glared at one another across growing chasms, including geographical (North and South), ideological (social responsibility and personal morality; abolition and slavery), theological (predestination and free will), denominational (local-church only and voluntary organizations), and ecclesiastical (frontier and urban). Perhaps the greatest point of agreement was the belief in public gospel proclamation, or evangelism. Yet, at this time, there was no certainty as to which version of Baptist evangelism would emerge as victor.

Finally, while Baptists in England and America expanded their horizons and while mission work in India progressed slowly (few converts were recorded in the initial decades of missionary endeavors), Baptists in the early nineteenth century began trickling into other nations. Johann Oncken became a pioneer of the spread of the Baptist faith worldwide when in 1834 he, his wife, and five others were baptized and formed the first Baptist church in Germany. Oncken pastored the Hamburg congregation, which is the oldest surviving congregation in Germany. And in what became a future pattern as Baptists later expanded into other countries, the early German Baptists experienced persecution by a government that did not recognize religious freedom.

Thus, for Baptists the year 1844 ended with promise and peril, hope and uncertainty. While unease permeated much of Baptist life internally, public vitality and diversity characterized the once persecuted denomination. Religious freedom remained only a partially-fulfilled dream in Europe, while in America Baptists wrestled with the overarching issue of human freedom.

THREE

GLOBAL EXPANSION AND AMERICAN CULTURE WARRIORS

1845-1924

Baptists of the late nineteenth and early twentieth centuries engaged a changing world from a perspective of strength and influence.

Their survival was now assured and their place in the world's religious landscape secured. From Europe Baptists spread outward worldwide, establishing local congregations, organizing denominationally, and championing freedom of religion. Meanwhile, Baptists in America reflected a nation in crisis; the northern brethren coalesced around abolitionist views while Baptists in the South marshaled biblical arguments to support slavery.

BAPTISTS OLD AND NEW
THE TRANSFORMATION OF BRITISH BAPTISTS
AND THE EMERGENCE OF GLOBAL BAPTISTS

British Baptists in the second half of the nineteenth century advanced slowly but steadily in the context of a nation that retained the trappings of an official state church. And intense controversy reshaped the Baptist landscape. The earlier successes of the Baptist Missionary Society (BSM) propelled that organization into a place of prominence in British Baptist life by mid-century, surpassing that of the Baptist Union, the national organization of Particular Baptists. Yet, by the end of the century, the Baptist Union re-exerted itself as it widened its theological tent to include General Baptists. Meanwhile, Baptists more fully embraced home missions in 1887 by creating a funding system to support Baptist churches in rural villages drained of city-bound citizens and to engage in social ministries (primarily temperance).

The steady progress of British Baptists found expression in congregational growth and expanding organizational entities that made few headlines and stirred little antipathy. Yet, the two most notable events of the era unfolded quickly and were bathed in hostility and bitterness; between 1887 and 1891, British Baptists battled over doctrine and reshaped their institutional direction.

During prior decades the Baptist Union had gradually refocused from a doctrinally-directed organization to one that embraced a primarily experiential and contextual view of Christianity. More specifically, contemporary biblical scholarship led Particular Baptists further away from their historically-strict Calvinistic foundation. The transition proceeded rather quietly until Charles H. Spurgeon (1834-1892), respected pastor of the large Metropolitan Tabernacle church and widely considered the greatest British Baptist preacher of the century, voiced opposition in March 1887 in his paper, the *Sword and the Trowel.* An article in the publication, titled "The Down Grade," provided the name for the controversy that erupted: The Down Grade Controversy, so called because some conservative Baptists viewed their denomination in a free fall away from moral and doctrinal purity.

Spurgeon's celebrity status in the British Baptist world immediately propelled him as the spokesperson for critics of denominational life. Although he fumed against declining local church prayer meetings and worldly ministers who embraced secular entertainment, the spear point of his complaints concerned encroaching liberalism in Baptist life. He identified as unorthodox the views of Christ, salvation, and the Bible espoused by some pastors. Yet, swift was the rebuke of British Baptist pastors, and for several months Spurgeon waged an uphill battle against unnamed "heretical" ministers. Unable to convince his fellow Baptists to turn the Baptist Union rightward, Spurgeon in November 1887 withdrew from both the Baptist Union and the venerable London Baptist Association.

Spurgeon angrily rebuffed attempts at reconciliation. When the Union in 1888 passed a stiff censure against him, the influential pastor battled all the harder against his perceived enemies. To his ongoing dismay, few churches followed his example of withdrawal from the Baptist Union. Adding further insult to injury, Spurgeon's rapid downfall resulted in the rise of John Clifford (1836-1923), a Methodist-turned-General-Baptist pastor, denominational statesman, social reformer, and soon the leading Baptist spokesman opposing Spurgeon.

Spurgeon never found satisfaction from the controversy, and his exit from the Baptist Union, followed by his death in 1892, aided reconciliation between Particular and General Baptists. With Clifford playing a pivotal role, the Baptist Union welcomed General Baptists into its membership in 1891, merging the individual pieces of their respective denominational organizations into unified entities. The century thus ended with growth in the numbers of British Baptist congregations against the backdrop of a fading Calvinism and an ascendant Arminianism.

British Baptist growth in this era included that of Scottish, Irish, and Welsh Baptists, all three of whom traced their roots to the seventeenth century. In the intervening years all had experienced some growth (with Welsh Baptists being the most vibrant, beneficiaries of European industrialization and urbanization) and lived through doctrinal controversies. In addition, some Welsh Baptists migrated to the Delaware/Jersey/Pennsylvania region of the New World and helped shape Baptist life there. Within their native lands, all three groups of Baptists formed national organizations in the late nineteenth century. By the time of the British Union merger in 1891, the Welsh Baptist denominational organization and operation paralleled that of English Baptists.

One Welsh Baptist whose ministry reflected the emerging, Arminian-influenced evangelistic emphasis of the early nineteenth century among British Baptists was Christmas Evans (1766-1838), considered by some as the greatest Welsh Baptist preacher. The "one-eyed Bunyan of Wales" (only one of his eyes was functional due to an accident in his youth), Evans preached in a loud, fiery voice, and was known for his exceptional story-telling ability. His preaching fame translated into regional influence, and for much of his later life Evans served as an advisor to and informal overseer of numerous Baptist congregations.

Elsewhere in Europe, the seeds of the Baptist faith sprouted in the late nineteenth century. In Germany, Johann Oncken remained the central Baptist fig-ure, establishing a publications ministry and providing educational opportunities

> In Germany, Johann Oncken remained the central Baptist figure, establishing a publications ministry and providing educational opportunities for German Baptists, while Hamburg (where Oncken pastored) in effect served as a center for European Baptists.

for German Baptists, while Hamburg (where Oncken pastored) in effect served as a center for European Baptists. The Union of Associated Churches of Baptized Christians in Germany and Denmark, founded in 1849 and modeled after America's Triennial Convention, met only in Hamburg until 1886.

Other European Baptists turned to Oncken for help in establishing churches. In the late 1840s and 1850s, he helped organize formal Baptist congregations in Switzerland, Austria, and the Netherlands (where Baptists had not existed since Thomas Helwys's congregation left in 1611). Baptists in all three nations grew and formed denominational structures in the decades following, despite religious persecution by the governments of Switzerland and Austria. Swiss Baptists in particular experienced notable growth, while Dutch Baptists remained much smaller in number and struggled with a variety of theological controversies. Oncken's influence also extended throughout much of the remainder of Europe.

In general, the Baptist presence in Europe followed a pattern of establishing formal congregations in the mid-nineteenth century, and denominationalism gradually emerged during the late nineteenth century. France proved to be an exception to this pattern; the first French Baptist congregation was established in 1835 and the first association in 1849. Baptists did not appear in Portugal and Belgium until near the end of the century. In addition, Russia was particularly receptive to the Baptist witness. Although Baptist establishment did not take place in Russia until 1867, early-twentieth-century Russia was home to the third largest population of Baptists worldwide.

Collectively, European Baptists of the era maintained an evangelistic emphasis. In some instances, they also embraced women deaconesses while commonly engaging in expanding social ministries, the latter a response to human needs in a modern world of industrial cities. In addition, religious liberty concerns remained front and center in much of the state-church-leaning European world. While persecution of Baptists did not approach the intensity or severity of earlier generations, many nineteenth-century European believers did not experience full freedom to practice their faith and express their views.

Outside of Europe, Baptists to the East and South grew slowly. While Baptists first appeared in Australia in the 1830s, the continent's vast size and status as a penal colony, plus spirited rivalry among the various English Baptists represented in the Commonwealth country, resulted in only a handful of congregations by the end of the century. Despite a century of missionary activity, Baptists remained scarce on the continents of Asia, Africa, and South America.

While early Baptist mission efforts in the Far East produced few converts, one stood out: Purushottam Chowdhari (1803-1890), an upper-caste West Bengali and a former Hindu who in 1833 converted to Christianity after reading, several years earlier, a Christian tract written by William Carey. Under the tutelage and encouragement of missionaries from the American Baptist Foreign Mission Society, Chowdhari became a preacher, evangelist, and pastor. As his ministry grew, he also became a prolific writer, authoring numerous books, pamphlets, and poems, in addition to composing over one hundred hymns, many yet sung by Indian Baptist congregations. By the time of Chowdhari's death, the Baptist presence demonstrated early signs of vitality in parts of India, especially among the lower castes.

The steady, if unspectacular, growth of international Baptists, against the backdrop of religious restrictions and cultural barriers, ushered in the era of global Baptists in the early twentieth century. Apart from the United States, Baptists at that time had a strong presence in Britain, Russia, and Canada (the latter claiming a Baptist presence since the 1770s), a diversity of thought and practice similar to that in Britain, and hundreds of congregations. The influence of British Baptists imprinted the faith worldwide, and thus, no one was surprised when British Baptists took the lead in forming a global Baptist body, the Baptist World Alliance (BWA), in 1905, with headquarters in London. Nazi bombs forced relocation of the organization to Washington, D.C., in 1941.

Although the idea for a worldwide Baptist organization can be traced to the early decades of Baptists, the occasional musings about such a possibility bore no fruition until modern communications and travel technologies of the early twentieth century provided infrastructure to make such an organization feasible. Editorials in 1903 and 1904 by Kentucky Baptist news editor John N. Prestridge (1833-1913) called for consideration of a worldwide Baptist "conference"; they piqued the interest of Baptist Union general secretary John H. Shakespeare (1857-1928), who also served as editor of the *Baptist Times and Freeman*. Shakespeare seized the initiative to make a global meeting of Baptists happen, rallying John Clifford and other English Baptist leaders to his cause. Collectively, these leaders extended an invitation to Baptists world-wide to gather in London in July 1905.

International fellowship was in the air, it seemed. Two months prior to the 1905 meeting of the world's Baptists, North American Baptists—black and white Americans and Canadians—met in St. Louis for fellowship and discussion. Although well-attended, the event was quickly overshadowed by the London gathering in July from which the Baptist World Alliance emerged. The BWA quickly drew Baptists of varying theological and denominational persuasions together for the common purposes of fellowship and advocacy for religious liberty, world peace, and hunger relief.

Despite the establishment of the BWA, the first quarter of the twentieth century witnessed challenging developments in the Baptist world. English Baptist growth crested, followed by internal dissension on theological and ecclesial fronts and the devastation wrought by the First World War. Meanwhile, Canadian and American Baptists experienced onslaughts of theological fundamentalism and the disunity of regionalism. Russian Baptists flourished before and immediately after World War I, prior to the Stalin era. Baptists in Australia yet had scarce representation across that vast land, although between 1891 and 1916 Baptist colleges were founded in Melbourne, Brisbane, and Sydney, respectively. Baptists in Africa and Asia, continents showing signs of rapid population growth, remained small in number, and their work was characterized more by Western missionary principles than native voices. Baptists in Latin America were so few as to be considered quite rare.

In short, while the BWA now gave voice to Baptists globally, Baptists outside of North America and Europe, few in number, found little visibility among the various religious views, cultural norms, and belief systems that dotted the globe. What attention they managed to obtain often resulted in persecution from without, even as a shortage of ministers and theological differences within stunted growth and effectiveness.

CULTURAL RESISTANCE, REFLECTION, AND ACCOMMODATION
THE STORY OF BAPTISTS IN AMERICA

While mid-nineteenth-century European Baptists slowly spread their faith across a traditionally theocratic landscape, the American Civil War reminded a secular nation of the religious underpinnings of its culture and society as the war years brought the country to its knees in collective (if disparate) prayer to God. Decades before the war began, unable to reconcile within their congregational ranks, Presbyterians (1837-1838), Methodists (1844) and Baptists (1845) split along North-South lines; in each case, Southerners took the initiative in breaking the ties. While theological and geographical differences played some role in the divisions, the overarching reason for the denominational splits was couched in a Protestant religion that mirrored the uneasy conscience of a nation struggling with human slavery. Coursing through congregational and denominational veins, the slavery and abolition debate led to the divisions of 1837-1845 that, in turn, sealed the fate of a nation hurtling toward self-inflicted tragedy.

Within the denomination displaying the greatest momentum in antebellum America, the rendering of the Baptist fabric reshaped the interplay of faith and society. Slavery transformed historic champions of the separation of church and state into opposing factions with evolving interpretations of what constituted church affairs and state matters. Baptists in the North, claiming the moniker "American Baptists" in 1845, turned to politics in an effort to eradicate slavery, a legally-established practice they viewed as unbiblical and immoral because it violated the basic human freedom ordained by God. Meanwhile, Baptists in the South, "Southern Baptists" as of 1845, argued that slavery, a biblical practice, remained solely a state matter. The church's only duty in regards to slavery, according to white southern believers, was to ensure that slaves were allowed to worship freely and were subject to humane treatment by their masters. Bodily freedom was ordained only for whites, the superior race established by God.

Baptists in America created new missions narratives in 1845. Northern

Baptist mission work, now freed from the criticisms posed by southern slave-holders, wove the theme of racial reconciliation into ministry both at home and in foreign lands. Southern Baptists, safe from abolitionist sentiment, turned to wealthy slaveholders to finance mission work in foreign lands. Prior to the Civil War, China and Liberia emerged as the two major mission fields of Southern Baptists, the latter including black American missionaries working among Africans. Baptists in the North and South financed their ventures by soliciting funds from interested local congregations and channeling the money through their respective mission boards. The Southern Baptist Convention (SBC) strove to create more centralized structures than the American Baptist "society" method of national organizations supported by interested individuals and congregations, but many decades would pass before the efforts bore full fruition.

From a larger perspective, Baptists North and South from 1845 to 1860, both claiming the biblical and moral high ground, and both preaching their respective messages of freedom, engaged in a culture war for the soul of America. Theologically, Northern Baptist opposition to slavery laid a long-term foundation for a contextual, non-literal interpretation of the Bible that focused on a twin mission of social action and evangelism. Southern Baptist embrace of slavery, on the other hand, elevated a selectively-literal interpretation of scripture that cemented a religion of personal responsibility at the individual level, affirmed God's sovereignty on a national and universal scale, and denied Christian responsibility for societal transformation.

The formation of Southern Baptists' first seminary, The Southern Baptist Theological Seminary (SBTS), founded in Greenville, South Carolina, in

1859 (relocated to Louisville, Kentucky, in 1877), served as a cultural and theological training ground for southern ministers. Thoroughly southern, the seminary affirmed white racial superiority and reflected Old School Presbyterian Calvinism, the dominant cultural and theological motifs of the antebellum South. Indeed, Southern Baptists turned to Presbyterian-trained theologians James P. Boyce (1827-1888, first president of SBTS) and Basil Manly, Jr. (1825-1892, author of the seminary's statement of faith, The Abstract of Principles) in the founding and shaping of theological studies.

Reverberating to this day, the two basic biblical worldviews of antebellum Northern and Southern Baptists—the former a contextual, this-worldly approach, and the latter a literal, other-worldly emphasis—reflect overarching patterns in Baptist life of the twenty-first century.

While the American Civil War put an end to slavery and elevated the legal status of African Americans to that of full citizens, the war and its aftermath temporarily reconstructed the Baptist landscape. White Southern Baptists, overall ardent supporters of the Confederacy, reeled from the devastation of a war-scarred land of destroyed church buildings, poverty, and a dearth of male members. Meanwhile, American Baptists, riding the coattails of a victorious North, streamed into the South and helped establish congregations and denominational organizations for freedmen. In response, Southern Baptists clung to, and refined, the emerging regional myth of the Lost Cause that explained the defeat as a noble and pious white southern culture victimized by the overwhelming force of an unrighteous, impure northern people.

Not surprisingly, African Americans interpreted the outcome of the Civil War as a victory for human morality and basic human freedom. Sometimes with the assistance of white Northerners and/or some white Southerners, and sometimes of their own initiatives, Baptist freedmen in the South followed the example of their northern brethren by creating their own churches and religious structures.

Formed in 1880 in Montgomery, Alabama, the Foreign Mission Baptist Convention became the first independent African American denomination in America. In 1886, the American National Baptist Convention was formed, followed by the Baptist National Education Convention in 1893. Collectively, the three organizations represented the primary interests of Black Baptists: missions, preaching, evangelism, and education, the last a priority because of a lack of educational opportunities among African Americans. In 1895, in Atlanta, the three organizations united under the umbrella of the National Baptist Convention, USA (NBC-USA).

The early years of the NBC-USA were marked by both expansion and controversy. Under the leadership of Elias C. Morris (1855-1922), a former slave who later became a minister and leader among Arkansas Baptists before assuming the position of the convention's first president, National Baptists in 1896 established the National Baptist Publication Board to supply church and Sunday School materials. The following year, some pastors left the convention and formed an alternative missionary organization, the Lott Carey Foreign Mission Convention. In 1915, pastors disgruntled over the role of the Publication Board formed a new convention, the National Baptist Convention of America. In short, competing visions of organizational structure and goals, rather then theological differences, provided fodder for controversy and division.

The upward, if halting, trajectory of black Baptists throughout America continued into the twentieth century, expressed in church, denominational, and missions growth. Meanwhile, Northern Baptists gradually refocused mission work in the West and education efforts in the East and Midwest while slowly disengaging from the South. At the same time, the legacy of early-nineteenth-century social activism shaped an increasingly holistic approach to ministry that contrasted with the individualistic evangelism of Southern Baptists. Also, in 1891, Southern Baptists established a denominational publishing house, the Baptist Sunday School Board (BSSB), to compete with the last remaining vestige of Northern Baptist influence in the South: the American Baptist Publication Society (ABPS).

By the end of the decade, the ABPS, and Northern Baptists at large, had effectively departed the South, thus reestablishing the geographical divisions among Baptists that had existed in the years prior to the Civil War. Clear lines of delineation allowed Baptists in the North to centralize denominational work and recast institutional vision. The American Baptist Education Society, formed in 1886, focused efforts and resources on The University of Chicago, founded in 1890 to provide theological training in the North. Reflecting their regionalism, Northern Baptists in 1908 consolidated their work under a new denominational name: the Northern Baptist Convention (NBC). Territorial agreements with the SBC, hammered out in 1909-1912, offered formal assurance that both groups would confine their efforts to their respective regions. Northern Free Will Baptists merged with the NBC in 1911. An NBC-wide fund-raising effort took place in 1919-1924. Northern Baptists also participated in the Interchurch World Movement, an ecumenical effort to help rebuild war-torn Europe and assist struggling post-war European Christians.

Freed from northern competition and riding the crest of a resurgent South, Southern Baptist missionary and evangelistic emphases on personal religion echoed turn-of-the-century white southern culture that welded Lost Cause mythology with urban industrialization. Thus, while Southern Baptists adopted modern business reforms to a greater extent than did Northern Baptists, race and gender hierarchies assured that white males remained firmly in control of an expanding, increasingly centralized New South denomination.

The changes took place quickly. In 1898, the SBC established a Centennial Committee to prepare for the challenges and opportunity of the coming century. A Committee on Co-operation was formed in 1901, with the goal of streamlining Southern Baptist organizations at the national and state levels. A Committee on Efficiency followed in 1914. That same year, Texas Baptists consolidated state work under an executive board. The SBC followed suit by creating a national Executive Committee in 1917, foreshadowing the first convention-wide fund-raising effort in 1919-1924 and the 1925 formation of the Cooperative Program, a unified and permanent denominational funding mechanism still in place. Collectively, these institutional changes showcased Southern Baptists' new reliance on "scientific management," the turn-of-the-century school of thought that applied the principles of scientific method to management in order to increase organizational function and efficiency.

In addition, the SBC established a Committee on Civic Righteousness (later renamed the Christian Life Commission, then the Ethics and Religious Liberty Commission) in 1907, an Education Commission in 1915, a convention-wide pension plan in 1918, and the Southern Baptist Historical

Society in 1922 (followed by a second founding in 1938). Finally, two new seminaries were founded during this time frame: Southwestern Baptist Theological Seminary (Texas) in 1908 and New Orleans Baptist Theological Seminary in 1917.

Meanwhile, Southern Baptist congregations embraced Sunday Schools; the percentage of churches with Sunday Schools rose from 25 to 84 percent between 1857 and 1926, with the bulk of the growth taking place from 1900 onward. In addition, the closing decades of the nineteenth century and early decades of the twentieth witnessed three overarching patterns of change at the local church level in the South: (1) demographically, the growth of urban churches outpaced that of rural congregations; (2) theologically, Calvinist dialogue largely disappeared at the congregational level (other than in Primitive Baptist churches), signaling the final triumph of revivalist evangelism and salvation as a personal decision rather than a divine, arbitrary appointment; and (3) ecclesiastically, discipline of church members virtually disappeared, a trend reflective of a denomination more embedded with surrounding culture than an oasis within a wilderness of sin.

The growth and transformation of local churches hinted at fundamental change in white Baptist life in the South and the United States at large. Transcending institutional growth, the story of Southern Baptists included individual personalities and grassroots controversies that played a defining role in a period of cultural warfare, which subtly challenged the past while constructing a foundation for radical future transformation. Among prominent individuals who shaped Baptists from the post-Civil War years to the 1920s were men and women, clergy and laity, orthodox believers and heretics, and Baptists and non-Baptists. Emerging narratives intersected theological, ecclesiastical, gender, and ideological axes, in some instances leading Baptists down new theological paths unknown to prior generations.

J. Nelson Darby (1800-1882), a priest in the Church of Ireland in the 1820s, was at the time an unlikely candidate to change the theological direction of Christianity. Yet, Darby in the 1830s formalized two theological concepts that, while originally considered heresy by Christendom, are today embraced as orthodoxy by many, if not most, evangelicals: Dispensationalism and the Rapture.

Darby crafted the theory of Dispensationalism to explain the working of God in the world. According to Darby's system, God's historical interaction with humans takes place in a series of seven chronological periods of time, or dispensations, the last of which corresponds with the end times, the theological study of which is called "eschatology." The final dispensation (and thus the history of the church), according to Darby, would culminate in a "secret rapture" (known simply as "the Rapture" in contemporary Christianity) in which Christ would return to earth and remove true believers from the world. Following the Rapture, a period of earthly tribulation would precede a 1,000-year earthly reign of Christ from the city of Jerusalem (the theological term for this is pre-millennialism).

Dismissed as heresy for decades by the Christian world at large, Darby's dispensational and rapture theories attracted some early followers, known as Plymouth Brethren. Yet, the post-American Civil War spiritual landscape, framed by devastation that challenged long-held Protestant confidence in post-millennialism (the belief that a 1,000-year figurative reign of Christ had begun with the advances and progress of the modern era) created a greater opening for Darbyism in the United States. Adopted by many American evangelicals increasingly disillusioned with the world at large, Darbyism became the first of three legs of the theological foundation of a new expression of Christianity that would transform early twentieth-century Baptists: fundamentalism, or religion defined by strict adherence to certain beliefs and principles fashioned in reaction to perceived theological lapses created by modern society and culture.

While Darbyism offered a new, overarching theological paradigm to explain and contextualize a modern world in disarray, two Presbyterian theologians, Charles A. Hodge (1797-1878, the theological grandfather of Southern Seminary) and Benjamin B. Warfield (1851-1921), provided a new construct of the Bible that repositioned holy writ in compatibility with modern truth. This reconstruction of the Bible was motivated by Charles Darwin's 1859 publication of *The Origin of the Species* (the famous scientific treatise that posited natural forces rather than God as the creator and sustainer of life) and the ascendancy of European "higher" biblical criticism (the utilization of modern literary analysis to question some traditional understandings of biblical truth). Cementing the primacy of rational thought over religious tradition as the source of truth, the twin developments set Hodge and Warfield about the task of revisioning biblical authority. Accepting the premise of the overarching validity of modern scientific inquiry and the attendant definition of truth as dependent upon quantifiable and precise data, the two theologians positioned scripture as scientific truth. In an 1881 article, "Inspiration," in the *Presbyterian Review*, they subsequently argued that the original biblical manuscripts ("autographa") were perfect and free of error in all matters.

By positioning the biblical text (although the original manuscripts were non-existent and their contents unknown) as perfect, Warfield and Hodge created the concept of "biblical inerrancy," a term that would be coined some years later. They thus staked a claim for the high ground on the playing field of modern truth. Nothing, in short, could match the precision and unerring, literal accuracy of the biblical text. Although developed independently of Darbyism, inerrancy ultimately found ready acceptance within the larger milieu of eschatologically-oriented, anti-modernist conservatives, thus becoming the second of the three legs of the founding of Christian fundamentalism.

With a worldview constructed and a religious text positioned as the source of all truth, the Presbyterians Lyman and Milton Stewart, the former a wealthy businessman who co-founded Union Oil (Unocal), provided the final leg upon which fundamentalism emerged. In 1910, the Presbyterian General Assembly, influenced by a series of Niagara Bible Conferences in 1878-1897 that had disseminated pre-millennial dispensationalist theology and biblical inerrancy, issued a response to modernism. The statement listed "five fundamentals" of orthodox faith: inerrancy of scriptures, virgin birth and deity of Jesus, substitutionary atonement, bodily resurrection of Christ, and the literalness of Christ's miracles. Upon these beliefs rested true Christianity.

Troubled by the scientific and liberal challenges to Christianity to which the five fundamentals responded, the Stewarts in 1910-1915 funded the publication of a series of pamphlets titled *The Fundamentals: Testimony to the Truth*. Comprised of ninety articles written by sixty-four authors, the pamphlets fleshed out a fundamentalist theology predicated on biblical inerrancy and pre-millennialism dispensationalism.

With the publication of these pamphlets, fundamentalism took formal shape as a new expression of Christianity and immediately caused theological discord among the ecumenically-minded, scholarly-oriented Northern Baptists. Evolutionary thought and biblical relativism had become the perceived heresies illustrative of the demon of liberalism despised by fundamentalists. William B. Riley (1861-1947), a fundamentalist and Baptist minister of a large congregation in Minneapolis, spearheaded the founding of the World Christian Fundamentals Association in 1919. Curtis L. Laws (1868-1946), editor of the popular Baptist *Watchman Examiner* newspaper, called for a conference on the "fundamentals" of the faith prior to the 1920 meeting of the NBC in Buffalo, New York. John R. Straton (1874-1929), pastor of Calvary Baptist Church in New York City, railed against liberalism through the medium of radio and published *The Fundamentalist*, a 1920s newspaper. A series of fundamentalist Baptist organizations quickly sprang up: the National Federation of the Fundamentalists of the Northern Baptists (1921), the Fundamentalist Fellowship (1921), and the Baptist Bible Union (1923).

Despite pressure from fundamentalists, the NBC maintained its historical non-creedal stance, traditional emphasis on freedom of conscience, increasingly moderate theology, and growing acceptance of modern scientific thought. Several prominent individuals played significant roles in refining and defending Northern Baptist identity during the era of emerging fundamentalism. William N. Clarke (1841-1912) and Augustus H. Strong (1836-1921), both serving as pastors, theologians, and professors, solidified a moderate to liberal imprint upon Northern Baptists, embracing biblical truth in the context of modern thought. Walter Rauschenbusch (1861-1918), author and professor at Rochester Theological Seminary and known as the "Father of the Social Gospel," emphasized Jesus' concern for the poor and oppressed and led Northern Baptists to engage the human problems brought about by northern industrialization. From a populist perspective, Harry Emerson Fosdick (1878-1969), professor at Union Theological Seminary and pastor of Riverside Church in New York, became the apologist for the moderate theology that came to characterize twentieth-century Northern Baptists. Helen Barrett Montgomery (1861-1934), Greek language scholar, social activist, president of the Women's American Baptist Foreign Mission Society (1914-1924), and president of the NBC (1921-1922), became the first woman elected president of a major Baptist denomination in the United States. From a moderate theological perspective, she resisted fundamentalism and championed freedom, in addition to serving as a pioneering advocate of gender equality.

Unsuccessful in their attempts to control Northern Baptists, many northern fundamentalists eventually left the denomination. The fundamentalist controversy, however, sapped the energy of Northern Baptists (later American Baptists), who limped along in terms of growth for the remainder of the century, while further embracing a gospel that balanced an individual evangelistic emphasis with social responsibility.

Southern Baptists also wrestled with fundamentalism in the 1920s. Edgar Y. Mullins (1860-1928), president of Southern Seminary, the SBC, and BWA, emerged as the denomination's leading spokesperson against insurgent fundamentalism and for freedom of conscience. His freedom-fueled *Axioms of Religion* (1908) offered a robust defense of the legacy of Roger Williams, Isaac Backus, and John Leland. Opposite Mullins stood J. Frank Norris (1877-1952), pastor of First Baptist Church of Fort Worth, Texas, who led the fundamentalist onslaught against the SBC. Despite a flamboyant and mean-spirited campaign against Southern Baptist leaders whom he considered too liberal (his slanderous accusations resulted in his expulsion from the Tarrant Baptist Association in 1922 and Texas Baptist Convention in 1924), Norris ultimately left the SBC of his own volition and became an independent Baptist.

For the SBC, the watershed moment in the fundamentalist battle proved to be the adoption of the Baptist Faith and Message (BFM) confessional statement at the convention's 1925 annual meeting. Although ideologically opposed by many Southern Baptists who, like Northern Baptists, had an aversion to adopting any human statement of faith, the impetus and ultimate acceptance of the BFM statement stemmed from efforts to combat fundamentalism. Affirming historic Baptist tenets, including freedom of conscience, the BFM positioned Southern Baptists as traditional Baptists espousing historically orthodox faith. Within this paradigm, diverse opinions were permitted, and scientific discoveries did not pose an inherent danger to faith. Dissatisfied with this response, fundamentalists felt marginalized and in the following years drifted away from the SBC.

The refusal of many Baptists to embrace fundamentalism reflected larger shifts at work in Baptist life. By the 1890s, formal Calvinism had quietly disappeared from Baptist life. Blunted by two eras of revivalism, a theologically-confusing Civil War, and an understanding of salvation that placed primacy upon human free will, the capriciousness of a God who randomly damned people to hell seemed out of context in a nation focused on freedom and uplift and within a publicly successful religion. As with fundamentalism, Baptists chose a path of moderation in deflecting Calvinism. The overarching principle of God's sovereignty was preserved, but it was a sovereignty that did not interfere with human freedom.

The theological moderation of the North and South was accompanied and enabled by changing gender roles and advancement in Baptist life. Having played lead roles in the northern antebellum abolitionist movement as well as assuming greater local church responsibilities in southern churches during and after the Civil War, Baptist women entered an era of growing empowerment. Whereas women deaconesses had not been uncommon in some areas of the South prior to the American Revolutionary War, a practice that largely disappeared during the revolutionary era, the re-ascendancy of Baptist women as leaders took place in the arenas of mission work and social ministries.

Lucy Peabody (1861-1949) of New York embodied the expanding missions and ministry opportunities afforded Northern Baptist women. A missionary to India from 1881 to 1886, Peabody returned to the states and in 1889 became the corresponding secretary of the Woman's Baptist Foreign Missionary Society. From then until 1927, she held a variety of denominational leadership positions and was a prolific author. She then withdrew from denominational service in protest of "modernist" theology, perhaps not fully appreciative that her own Baptist journey reflected modernist views of women's roles.

Among Southern Baptists, the life of Lottie Moon (1840-1912) became legendary because of her singular devotion to missions. Her work in China from 1873 until her death encompassed a variety of ministries among poverty-stricken nationals. While many Southern Baptist preachers in the states grumbled about her role as a preacher, Moon's devotion to the mission cause arguably transformed her into the most well-known Southern Baptist of the late nineteenth century. Although never serving in a denominational leadership role, her mission service inspired the formation of the national Woman's Missionary Union (WMU) in 1888, an SBC auxiliary that has provided significant funding for Southern Baptist missions until the present. While the WMU in its early years made no effort to support egalitarian gender roles, it did provide women a new voice and an elevated role within an otherwise male-dominated religious world.

Complementing Moon, Annie Armstrong (1850-1938), in her young years involved in mission work among internationals in Baltimore, led in creating WMU and served as the organization's first leader, at her own expense. A successful administrator and fund-raiser, Armstrong remained conservative in theology, opposing women as congregational leaders. Her refusal to support the formal training of women as missionaries eventually led to her resignation from the WMU, although not before establishing the long-term viability of the organization.

Many African American Baptist women also served as leaders. One exceptional woman, Nannie Helen Burroughs (1879-1961), became a leader among African American Baptists as her life and ministry intersected missions work, denominational service, and the national women's movement. The daughter of former slaves, Burroughs received formal training in business and domestic science and in 1896 helped establish the National Association of Colored Women. She also worked as an editor, and beginning in 1900 served as a secretary of the Foreign Mission Board of the National Baptist Convention. In addition, she founded, in 1909, the National Training School for Women and Girls in Washington, D.C., an organization dedicated to instilling pride in black women and helping students become respectable and contributing members of society.

Aside from mission service and denominational leadership, Baptist women took leadership roles in the Sunday School, temperance, prohibition, and anti-child-labor-law movements. The growth of Baptist Sunday Schools, confined in the nineteenth century to children, in the post-Civil War era resulted directly from the work of women, who served as both advocates and teachers. Founded in 1873, the Woman's Christian Temperance Union, the culmination of local-ized temperance societies founded as early as the 1830s, stood as the effort of Christian feminists dedicated to combating the influence of alcohol within families and society on a national scale. Although Baptist women were not among the leaders of the union, and many, if not most, Baptist churches still served wine for communion, by the turn of the century Baptist women were commonly involved in women's temperance societies. Their influence resulted in a Baptist movement against alcohol that by the 1920s publicly positioned many Baptists as teetotalers and prohibitionists. In addition, in the early decades of the twentieth century, Baptist women increasingly embraced anti-child-labor campaigns. In the South, a progressive WMU engaged social ministries, balancing evangelism with community uplift.

The advance of women in Baptist life of this era did not come without op-position: Baptist life (white and black, North and South) remained a male-dominated narrative within a paternal-istic American society; and apart from missions work and social ministry, few opportunities were afforded the female gender. Although northern women enjoyed fewer restrictions than their counterparts living within the tightly-structured gender roles of southern states, Baptist pulpits remained off lim-its in local congregations. In addition, women's public voices within denomi-national organizations remained almost exclusively confined to women's circles. Even the national women's suffrage

The advance of women in Baptist life of this era did not come without opposition: Baptist life (white and black, North and South) remained a male-dominated narrative within a paternalistic American society; and apart from missions work and social ministry, few opportunities were afforded the female gender.

movement, culminating in the Nineteenth Amendment to the U. S. Constitution (1920) allowing women the right to vote, failed to significantly dent gender biases in Baptist life. Nonetheless, within their expanding, yet limited, spheres, many Baptist women of the late nineteenth and early twentieth centuries learned organizational and communication skills that enabled later generations to expand women's roles much further.

While theological battles and cautious gender advancement characterized one aspect of the culture wars, ecclesiastical conflicts also consumed Baptists during much of this time. From the 1850s until the end of the century, Baptists experienced an intense struggle to define the concept of "church." At a time when American Protestants offered competing claims for the title of most authentic faith tradition, some Baptists known as "Landmarkers" went to great lengths to "prove" the superiority of the Baptist faith.

Borrowing a page from Primitive, anti-missions Baptists, Landmarkers insisted that "church" existed only at the congregational level. In addition, only Baptist churches were authentic churches, established by Jesus and the apostles through an unbroken succession of true churches that existed since the time of Christ. This view of Baptist origins denied that Baptists originated from the English Separatist wing of the Church of England that had emerged from the Roman Catholic Church; to Landmarkers, as to many Baptists of that era, Catholics were not genuine Christians. Although not based within historical reality, Baptist "sucessionism" served the questionable purpose of positing Baptists as the original Christians who had maintained the one true faith since the time of Christ.

Landmarkism also taught that the biblical words "kingdom" and "church" were synonymous, and that the Kingdom of God was comprised of the sum total of Baptist churches. Finally, since only Baptist congregations were true churches, Landmarkers also asserted that non-Baptists were not welcome in Baptist pulpits, that only persons immersed in Baptist churches were truly saved, and that non-Baptists were not allowed to participate in communion (the practice of which was valid only if it took place within a local Baptist congregation).

Popular in some rural areas of the Southeast and Southwest, the three ideological leaders of Landmarkism were Southerners. James R. Graves (1820-1893), considered the "father" of the movement, used his position as editor of the *Tennessee Baptist* newspaper to popularize Landmarkism. He also wrote several books and pamphlets on the subject, as did James M. Pendleton (1811-1891), a pastor in Bowling Green, Kentucky, who advocated Landmark views through his popular 1867 *Church Manual.* A. C. Dayton (1813-1865), pastor and Southern Baptist denominational leader in Tennessee and Georgia, authored numerous treatises espousing Landmarkism, including a popular novel, *Theodosia Ernest.*

Together, these three men provided Landmarkism with momentum and ensured public visibility. Their passing, however, left the movement in a vulnerable position. The end of an era came paradoxically as rural Landmark congregations, after forcing the 1898 resignation of Southern Seminary's president William H. Whitsitt (1841-1911) over his contention that Baptists originated in the early 1600s, quietly withdrew among themselves. Some Landmark congregations yet exist, clustered primarily in the Southwest and Appalachian regions of the Southeast.

While Baptist theological, gender, and ecclesiological transformations played out against the backdrop of an increasingly diverse cultural landscape that challenged religious and societal norms, two traditional Baptist themes remained steadfast: a commitment to religious liberty and church state separation, and the centrality of preaching.

Despite intense theological conflict, Baptists of all persuasions remained ardent and vocal advocates of religious liberty and separation of church and state. Even as some Baptists battled against perceived evils of cultural and scientific modernism, liberal and fundamentalist Baptists alike found common ground in George W. Truett's (1867-1944) May 16, 1920, religious liberty speech on the steps of the nation's Capitol. "The chiefest contribution that America has thus far made to the civilization," the former North Carolina farm boy who now served as pastor of the prestigious First Baptist Church of Dallas, declared, was the Baptist-inspired "contribution of religious liberty." He continued, "Freedom of conscience, unlimited freedom of mind, was from the first the trophy of the Baptists." And "the struggle waged by our Baptist forefathers" ensured "that church and state must in this land be forever separate and free, that neither must ever trespass upon the distinctive functions of the other."

Truett also represented the Baptist commitment to preaching, standing among the greatest Baptist preachers of his era in America. He shared the spotlight with such men as the previously mentioned Harry Emerson Fosdick, a Northern Baptist and considered by some as the greatest American preacher ever; John Jasper (1812-1901), a former slave who became an African American evangelist and founded the Sixth Mount Zion Baptist Church in Richmond in 1867, became a leader in the community of Richmond, and is remembered as the greatest black Baptist preacher and orator of the late nineteenth century; and Benjamin H. Carroll (1843-1914), a Mississippian who pastored the First Baptist Church of Waco, Texas, from 1871 to 1899 and transformed the congregation into a leading church in the state, taught at Baylor, was a prominent denominational figure in Texas Baptist life, and helped found Southwestern Baptist Theological Seminary.

In summary, the antebellum to early-twentieth-century era witnessed the tumultuous coming-of-age of the historical freedom fighters known as Baptists. Perhaps few seventeenth- and eighteenth-century Baptists could have envisioned the successes and broad public influence that their spiritual descendants would achieve. Fewer still might have anticipated the internal fragmentation and widespread cultural engagement—whether in terms of reflecting or combating culture—that came to characterize late-nineteenth- and early-twentieth-century Baptists. Yet, such entanglement was inevitable as individual Baptists became prominent members of society, congregations assumed more visible roles within their respective communities, and denominational organizations matured and commanded sizeable resources and regional influence. And while most Baptists remained committed to religious liberty and separation of church and state into the twentieth century, fundamentalist assaults upon denominational life raised the question of whether freedom of conscience could be maintained in a modern Baptist world increasingly defined by national institutions and diverging ideologies.

FOUR

NAVIGATING
A NEW WORLD

1925-1963

Baptists experienced geographical,
institutional, ideological, and doctrinal
transformations in 1925-1963. Western
euphoria of the early 1920s proved short-
lived. By the end of the decade, the
hope following the first global war, a
conflict so vast in scope and devastation
that it became known as the War to End
All Wars, gave way to perplexing and
troubling developments worldwide.

In Eastern Europe, the Russian Civil War concluded in 1923 with the Bolshevik Party securely in power; the era of communism had arrived, to the dismay and fear of Western democracies. Meanwhile, Germany, restless and resentful under post-World War I penalties, witnessed a renewed nationalist movement that grew increasingly militant in the latter half of the decade. As if these troubling developments were not enough, the United States plunged into economic disarray when the stock market crashed on October 29, 1929. The resulting financial crisis quickly spread throughout the world.

The decades following bore witness to one global crisis after another: the Great Depression and rise of Nazi Germany in the 1930s, World War II and the beginning of the Cold War in the 1940s, the Korean War and the threat of nuclear annihilation in the 1950s, and the Vietnam War and nuclear brinksmanship in the 1960s. The common thread throughout much of the era proved to be communism. While Hitler and Nazism suffered total defeat in the culmination of World War II, communism emerged from the second global war as a well-armed Eastern European and Asian political ideology that threatened Western democracies and freedom, instilled fear in the hearts of American citizens, and ushered in a new wave of Christian persecution.

During this era, the Baptist story became increasingly complicated and nuanced even as Baptists as a whole experienced unparalleled growth. Decline and/or persecution characterized Baptists in Britain, Germany, the Soviet Union, Australia, Korea, and China. At the same time, Baptists in the Southern Hemisphere experienced greater growth than ever. Canadian and American Baptists also increased in numbers and erased internal geographical boundaries, even while fracturing along doctrinal demarcation lines as religious fundamentalism, fueled by fear of and growing opposition to "godless" communism without and theological impurity within, watered and nurtured the seeds of religio-cultural revolution. At the same time, in the United States Baptists white and black confronted longstanding social structures infused with racial prejudice.

GLOBAL BAPTISTS
A BATTERED WITNESS AND A BRAVE NEW FAITH

The story of Baptists outside the United States from the late 1920s to the early 1960s unfolded in numerous crosscurrents and revealed the vitality, challenges, and diversity present within a denomination comprised of over one hundred distinct groupings worldwide.

> The story of Baptists outside the United States from the late 1920s to the early 1960s unfolded in numerous crosscurrents and revealed the vitality, challenges, and diversity present within a denomination comprised of over one hundred distinct groupings worldwide.

To begin with, World War II and the Cold War dramatically reconfigured the European Baptist landscape, further interrupting church life and reducing many church buildings to ashes at a time of congregational decline otherwise. Even before warfare broke out, the rise of Hitler and Nazism in the 1930s generated tensions among Baptists. While some German Baptists never embraced Nazism (and suffered the consequences), most accommodated the Nazi Party, in many instances viewing Nazism as a lesser evil than communism, then threatening from the East.

Like many other Christians, some Baptists were drawn to a Nazi ideology publicly constructed upon faith and patriotism. The Fuhrer's party professed a high moral ground by paying homage to the nation's patron saint (Luther); melded conservative Christian language and ideology with nationalism; and enacted laws designed to ensure the morality of public life and purity of purpose. A growing awareness that the locus of Hitler's crusade for morality and purity involved the elevation of the Aryan race and the removal of Jews, homosexuals, and intellectual liberals from society caused mild discomfort, mitigated by the legacy of Luther's anti-Semitism. By the time many German Baptists realized the full extent of Hitler's evil intentions—morally and militarily—the compromises were too great and the time too late. While Baptists of post-war Britain, France, and Europe's smaller nations spent decades rebuilding, German Baptists struggled with both national devastation and psychological angst.

Yet, Nazism, for all its evil, killing, deception, and intensity, proved but a passing problem for the Baptists of Europe. Within the larger narrative that began unfolding in the 1930s, Western democracy suffered duel sieges from fascism (authoritarian nationalism) and Soviet communism. For a period of time, all of Europe seemed destined to be ruled by one of the two ideologies. Since fascism accommodated religious institutions, albeit with restrictions, while communism forbade all religious expression, many Baptists and other European Christians under siege opted for fascism. While the end of World War II snuffed out the fascist threat, it also ushered in communist ascendancy in Eastern Europe and Asia and threatened the vitality of Christianity across much of the globe.

The post-war religious liberty landscape on planet Earth represented a new crisis brought about by the vast geographical presence commanded by the Soviet Union and China. To the surprise of many, the Soviet Union somewhat relaxed restrictions on religious expressions; evangelicals, into which Baptists were lumped, were allowed to have a limited presence in the Soviet bloc, absent foreign influence and under the watchful eye of the government. China, on the other hand, transitioned from limited religious tolerance to formal persecution. In addition to forbidding foreign involvement and expelling all western missionaries, the Chinese government in the 1950s nationalized all things religious and demanded public loyalty from church leaders. The persecution grew even more intense in the following decade; all religious institutions were dismantled, forcing Christians to meet secretly underground. Thereafter, while a few churches yet remained in the growing communist sphere, the few religious institutions permitted existed in isolation and under strict government control, with individual Christians (particularly those assembling unlawfully) subject to imprisonment, labor camps, or death.

Mounting religious persecution during this era did not go unnoticed by the Baptist World Alliance. With the 1928 hiring of the forward-looking English Baptist James H. Rushbrooke (1870-1947) as its first full-time secretary, the BWA swung into full stride even as Hitler consolidated power in Germany. Rushbrooke had led the BWA to institute regional gatherings beginning in 1926, and Secretary Rushbrooke now led the Alliance in publicly advocating religious freedom for persecuted Romanian and Russian Baptists. The BWA's efforts, however, came up empty. Both the Soviet Union and the United States simply ignored pleas for religious freedom in the communist sphere.

The year 1934 presented an opportunity for the Baptist World Congress to address the world's other menace, Nazism. Meeting in Berlin, European and American Baptist leaders attended the event with unease. Welcomed by Hitler and the Nazi Party and assured by German Baptist leaders of the Nazis' good intentions, delegates dismissed concerns and spoke lightly of Nazism and favorably of their German Baptist brethren, offering moral support during the difficult times.

Five years later, meeting in Atlanta, BWA attendees—other than the German delegation that still defended passivism as the best response to Hitler—focused on the subject of war, declaring nationalism and racial prejudice to be primary moral issues. African American participation highlighted the meeting, and religious persecution in communist nations remained an overarching concern. The following year, as war ravaged the globe, the BWA shifted gears and placed greater emphasis on world relief efforts, a mission that lasted well into the post-war rebuilding years. In addition, the BWA led the way in helping struggling post-war European Baptists form unions (Austrian and Italian Baptists, for example, established initial institutions), work together, and fight for religious liberty (including in Spain and Romania). BWA efforts on behalf of European Baptists paved the way for the 1950 formation of the European Baptist Federation, a platform for mutual cooperation and encouragement.

Nonetheless, struggle characterized European Baptists into the 1960s.

While the formation of The Baptist Theological Seminary in Switzerland in 1949 marked a high point for European Baptists, larger European Baptist life focused on efforts to gain formal denominational recognition and establish a viable presence within the context of limited religious toleration and growing continental secularism. The crafting of confessions of faith characterized the era. In order to meet government regulations, many European Baptist groups were forced to pen faith statements. Other Baptist groups created confessions in the wake of internal divisions or simply in order to instruct the faithful. Finally, the backdrop of European secularism dulled the evangelical witness of Baptists, resulted in increased ecumenism in Western Europe, and limited sectarian educational opportunities.

Yet, the paralysis in Western Europe and persecutions in the East represented only part of the story of international Baptists. A 3,000-voice Brazilian Baptist choir, leading worship for the 1960 Baptist World Congress meeting—the tenth such meeting of the Congress—signaled the dawning of a new era in Baptist life. For the first time, the event was held outside of Europe and North America. Rio de Janeiro provided the backdrop, and attendance was greater than at any meeting ever held outside the United States. Of the nearly 13,000 delegates present, 10,000 were Brazilians.

This World Congress echoed a global shift to the Southern Hemisphere that was taking place among Baptists. Although the hemispheric shift would not solidify until several decades later, Baptist momentum in Ethiopia, Nigeria, Mexico, and Brazil, among other nations, offered notable contrast to the weakened positions of the faithful in Europe. The Baptist trajectory in many nations of the Southern Hemisphere by 1960 included the rapidly increasing numbers of congregations, growth in total church membership, and the development of regional and national denominational organizations. Religious restrictions and persecutions in Catholic and Muslim nations, while contributing to minimal advance in some countries, could not stem the Baptist tide.

To be certain, Western Baptists could claim no small amount of credit for successes in the global south; missionary efforts on the part of European and American Baptists helped lay the groundwork for the growth of African and Latin American believers. In particular, missionaries from the United States assisted in preaching the gospel, building churches, engaging social ministries, and training indigenous leaders. Beginning in the 1940s, independent, fundamentalist Baptist missionaries joined Southern and Northern Baptists in Latin and African nations. They brought a Western-influenced Christian faith that at times displayed little respect for local culture and customs, while missionaries and missionary agencies and boards alike did little to encourage independence among nationals. In short, early twentieth-century mission efforts evidenced both positive and negative results.

Accordingly, the few thousand Baptists from the Northern Hemisphere who attended the 1960 Congress in Rio de Janeiro caught a glimpse of Latin Baptists treading a path away from dependence on Western Christian traditions and into possession of a regional Baptist faith. Although not entirely understood or fully appreciated at the time, this path would soon come to reflect the transformation of global Baptists at large as nationals across the Southern Hemisphere responded to the gospel of Christ and the message of freedom.

Finally, during this time of transformation, a number of individuals appearing on the international stage became Baptist legends in their respective corners of the world, including Baptist minister-turned-politician Tommy Douglas (1904-1986). Influenced by the Social Gospel while in seminary and pastoral ministry, Douglas became premier of Saskatchewan (1944-1961) and an ardent advocate of universal health care and basic human rights. His leadership resulted in the Saskatchewan Bill of Rights (1947) and creation of Canada's public health care system (1962). In 2004, Douglas was voted by Canadians as the greatest Canadian of all time.

Down Under, Frank W. Boreham (1871-1959) is considered by some as the best Australian Baptist preacher ever. Spurgeon's last student, Boreham pastored in New Zealand and Australia in 1894-1928. Afterward, when not preaching or writing in Australia, he traveled the world as an itinerant preacher. Recognized during his lifetime by Queen Elizabeth for his preaching ministry, Boreham left a legacy of numerous books, while his accomplishments inspired the creation of several Boreham heritage centers.

Baptist diversity, in short, expanded on a global level against the backdrop of troubled times. By the early 1960s, Baptists around the world spoke hundreds of languages and framed their faith through a multitude of cultural, social, and doctrinal lenses.

BAPTISTS IN AMERICA
REEVALUATING BAPTIST IDENTITY

The story of Baptists in the United States from the late 1920s to the early 1960s unfolded in numerous crosscurrents and revealed the vitality, challenges, and diversity within a denomination reevaluating its identity. Although broadly characterized by a stagnant Northern Baptist Convention and an ascendant Southern Baptist Convention, some of the most significant developments originated from independent, fundamentalist Baptists who transitioned from an exclusively militant, enclave mentality to a fractured grouping sharing similar theology but widely disparate methodology that produced both evangelist Billy Graham and political activist Jerry Falwell (1933-2007). In addition, African American Baptists entered the 1960s more energized than ever, a result of civil rights successes that owed much to the courage and vision of Martin Luther King, Jr. (1929-1968), as well as many other African American ministers and laypersons, both male and female.

During this era, Northern and Southern Baptists reached the centennial anniversary of their 1845 split. Over the course of those one hundred years, the two groups at times found their trajectories intertwined, while in other instances their differences remained stark and unmistakable. Whereas 1845 represented a denominational split, not until the 1890s, when Southern Baptists finally swung their literature loyalties to the Southern Baptist Sunday School Board, did Baptists in the North and South sever the final institutional threads between the two bodies. Yet, within a decade, Baptists in the North claimed the institutional language of Southern Baptists, as evidenced by their adoption of a new name, Northern Baptist Convention. Both groups then bore a full measure of the fundamentalist onslaught in the 1920s, and both successfully repelled fundamentalism, albeit in different ways. The more social ministry-oriented Northern Baptists succeeded by reaffirming the historical Baptist position of no creeds but the Bible, while evangelistic-centered Southern Baptists, in an effort to placate fundamentalists, reached back in time to early Baptists' affinity for non-binding confessions of faith and—working from the 1833 moderately Calvinistic New Hampshire Confession—crafted the 1925 Baptist Faith and Message.

Gradually tacking to the theological left from the 1920s onward, Northern Baptists, despite repelling fundamentalism, struggled to retain momentum in numerical growth. In 1926, they affirmed the necessity of baptism by immersion as a qualifier for participation in annual meetings, but fundamentalists continued sniping from within into the 1940s (particularly focusing on denominational publications), before finally splintering into separate organizations. In 1933, the Baptist Bible Union, formed a decade earlier to give voice to fundamentalist Baptists and now comprised of several hundred congregations, separated from Northern Baptists and took the name General Association of Regular Baptist Churches (GARBC). A second fundamentalist splinter group, tracing its roots to the 1920 founding of the Fundamentalist Fellowship of Northern Baptists, remained a faction within Northern Baptist life until the 1940s. Unsuccessful in forcing the NBC to adopt conservative requirements for mission service, the Fundamentalist Fellowship in 1947 formed the Conservative Baptist Association (CBA), and in 1951 severed all remaining ties to Northern Baptists. In a larger context, the two groups (including their precursors) advocated strict separation from culture, in effect creating an alternative narrative consisting of strict dress codes, social norms, and educational indoctrination.

The GARBC and CBA represented larger trends in fundamentalist Baptist life: continual fragmentation and the birthing of myriads of new groups with ever-changing (and lengthy) names. J. Frank Norris's fundamentalism resulted in the formation of the Premillennial Missionary Baptist Fellowship in 1933, five years later renamed the World Fundamental Baptist Missionary Fellowship (WFBMF). In 1950, the WFBMF split into two separate groups: the World Baptist Fellowship and the Baptist Bible Fellowship

International (BBFI). Well-known fundamentalist pastor Jerry Falwell began his ministry within the BBFI with the founding of Thomas Road Baptist Church in Lynchburg, Virginia, in 1956. The twentieth century's most visible Baptist, evangelist Billy Graham was a prodigy of Baptist fundamentalist William Riley. Graham, however, eventually become a representative of a toned-down version of fundamentalism known as neo-evangelicalism, a term coined in 1947 to describe a new breed of fundamentalists who engaged, rather than remained separate from, culture and society. Unlike most fundamentalist Baptists, Graham in the late fifties and sixties took public stances against racial segregation.

Meanwhile, secular trends emerging in America's large cities impacted the urban North far more than they did the rural South, draining Northern Baptist membership from the far left even as the far rightward exodus continued on the other end of the theological spectrum. As if theological challenges were not enough, Northern Baptists also found themselves in a geographically-induced vise as Southern Baptists in the 1940s expanded into northern territory, in violation of earlier "comity" agreements prohibiting territorial overlapping. Acting to defend their home turf, Northern Baptists changed names in 1950, adopting the inclusive title of American Baptist Convention (ABC). The theme of inclusion also bore evidence in a broader, growing ecumenism that led to membership in the liberal World Council of Churches, further alienating some within the denomination's remaining conservative contingent.

In short, from the 1920s through the early 1950s, the internal dynamics of Northern/American Baptist life resulted in a series of significant challenges intruding from seemingly all directions. Overwhelmed and inundated, American Baptists of the fifties, while once a vibrant Baptist witness in the North and now claiming the entire nation as their home turf, struggled with an identity crisis. Worse yet, during the decade, while other Christian groups experienced rapid growth (and religious affiliation in America rose above 60 percent for the first time), fueled by record marriages and births and subsequent suburban young families with newfound appreciation for the stabilizing influence of church life, American Baptists lost members. By the time American Baptists relocated their headquarters to Valley Forge, Pennsylvania, in 1960, the downturn was quite pronounced and worrisome to denominational leaders.

Despite multi-dimensional challenges, Northern/American Baptists experienced some notable advances and triumphs. A decrease in the number of foreign missionaries corresponded with a new focus on training national ministers and establishing national congregations, both of which witnessed significant numerical growth. On the home front, Northern Baptists supplied more chaplains during World War II than any other denomination except Methodists, while taking the lead among all denominations in ministering to non-English-speaking immigrants. In 1957, Japanese-American Jitsuo Morikawa (1912-1987) assumed the helm of the Division of Evangelism of the Home Mission Society, and in the years following emphasized a more balanced approach to evangelism that incorporated social action.

In addition, Northern/American Baptists remained focused on ministerial education. While the University of Chicago represented the liberal side of the denomination, Eastern Baptist Theological Seminary, founded in Philadelphia in 1925 in response to fundamentalist criticisms, provided more conservative theological training and evangelistic emphasis. In the years following, Northern/American Baptists systematically sought to increase educational standards and more fully meet the needs of congregations, efforts that met with limited success.

Finally, American Baptists in the 1950s and early 1960s advocated for civil rights from a denominational pulpit, although many congregations remained segregated. Among early advocates of racial reconciliation was Howard Thurman (1900-1981), the grandson of a slave, graduate of American Baptists' Colgate Rochester-Crozer Divinity School, and dean of chapel at Howard University in Washington, D.C., all prior to co-founding the racially integrated, cultural Church for the Fellowship of All Peoples in San Francisco in 1944. In 1953, Thurman became the dean of chapel at Boston University, the first tenured African American chapel dean at a majority-white university.

While Northern/American Baptists struggled to understand their identity, Southern Baptists fine-tuned their cultural affinity with the region of their birth. *Baltimore Sun* religion and social columnist and editor Henry L. Mencken (1880-1956) succinctly captured the essence of the relationship between Baptists and the South when in 1924 he coined the term "Bible Belt." From Texas in the Southwest, Virginia in the Upper South, and Florida in the Southeast, the SBC of the mid-1920s had no religious equal in the states of the old Confederacy. A literal Bible, racial divisions, tenant farming, and limited emphasis on education remained little-changed since the Civil War era. Yet, a New South now existed alongside the old, expressed in progressive urban cities, modernized textile and mining industries, mechanized farm equipment, and a rising professional and business class.

Rather than working against Southern Baptists, the changing South propelled its dominant faith into an even greater seat of influence. Reaching both backward and forward, the 1925 Baptist Faith and Message statement represented conservative doctrinal continuity (and neutralized fundamentalist critics), while the 1925 formation of the SBC Cooperative Program tacked the convention New South-ward, mirroring the professionalism and business practices of the region's urban centers. The convention's boards and agencies, now beneficiaries of unified funding, and an SBC anchored in the region's ideological past and steered by southern progressive methodologies seemed poised for new heights.

The Great Depression, however, temporarily delayed Southern Baptists' glory days. Churches squeezed by the financial crisis proved unable to fully fund denominational goals. The most affected agency, the Home Mission Board, teetered on bankruptcy, victimized by both the Depression and an embezzlement scandal. To a lesser degree, the Foreign Mission Board suffered, as receipts dropped to about half of 1920 levels and missionary numbers stagnated. If not for the efforts of Woman's Missionary Union, whose members under the leadership of Kathleen Mallory (executive secretary from 1912-1948) personally raised enough funding to salvage the HMB and keep the FMB afloat, the missionary efforts of Southern Baptists—the locus and nexus of the denomination—could well have been severally crippled for decades. Even so, the mission boards did not fully recover until the post-war era.

To Selma, Alabama, native Mallory (1879-1954) may belong the distinction of being the single individual who most prepared Southern Baptists for the denomination's "golden age" in the 1950s. Her helm at the WMU spanned that of five FMB heads and three HMB directors, while none excelled her in leadership effectiveness. Known as "the sweetheart of Southern Baptists," Mallory relocated WMU headquarters from Baltimore to the city of Birmingham, Alabama, rescued the future of the mission boards, and led WMU to a four-fold increase in membership. A prolific writer and social reformer, her passions paralleled those of Social Gospel advocate Walter Rauschenbusch, who frequently spoke at annual WMU conventions. Yet, Mallory's national position, organizational leadership skills, and public visibility throughout Southern Baptist life allowed her to influence the direction of the denomination beyond that of Rauschenbusch, as she led hundreds of thousands of Southern Baptist women within thousands of local church organizations to embrace social ministries (denominational, ecumenical, and secular) to women, the urban poor, and immigrants. By the time of Mallory's retirement in 1948, Southern Baptists, in addition to being on solid financial ground, had transitioned into an era of denominational social progressivism heretofore unknown.

While Mallory's leadership proved critical to the institutional survival and socially progressive transformation of the SBC, Arthur Flake (1862-1952) enabled congregational growth, furthered loyalty to the SBC, and influenced the ideological composition of Southern Baptists. In 1925, most Baptist Sunday School classes remained limited to children. But Flake, a native Texan serving as an administrator with the Baptist Sunday School Board (a post he assumed in 1920), had other ideas. His 1922 book, *Building a Standard Sunday School*, contained a "Fivefold Formula" for church growth based on adult Sunday School. Many congregations in the late 1920s and following, eager for numerical growth, adopted the formula, which essentially positioned adult Sunday School as a recruiting tool to attract new members. Widely successful in expanding church rolls, Flake's Sunday School-centric church growth strategy remains popular to this day in some Baptist congregations and beyond.

In addition to fostering church growth, Flake's success in positioning adult Sunday School as a primary congregational component paved the way for the Baptist Sunday School Board to achieve a nearly universal presence within Southern Baptist congregations. The shared experience of BSSB literature in local churches, in turn, led to greater denominational loyalty at the congregational level. Sunday School lessons became the source of common Bible study within congregations, while Board literature in general generated continuity among thousands of local churches. Training Union, begun in 1934 and utilized within congregations on Sunday nights, focused on Baptist history, distinctives, and beliefs. Collectively, Sunday School and Training Union melded Baptist identity with institutional vision within congregations.

The continuity represented by Flake and change exemplified by Mallory thus existed side-by-side within local congregations and denominational life. At the same time, the white South remained socially, culturally, and theologically conservative; progressive reforms were muted, racial tensions magnified, and theological discourse dated compared to that of the North. Denominational leadership, increasingly progressive (albeit cautiously) in the post-war years, represented 7 million church members in 27,000 churches by 1950, more than double thirty years earlier. Southern Baptists, in short, reached a pinnacle of numerical growth despite enduring the denomination's greatest financial challenges since the Civil War.

Any remaining denominational troubles seemingly evaporated in the post-war years. Whereas the 1950s represented a notable downturn for American Baptists, Southern Baptist growth in the late 1940s and 1950s benefited from a south-wide population boom and reflected a Cold War white conservatism driven by fears of communism that, in turn, contributed to a general religious revival. Already the largest faith group within their geographical home, Southern Baptists further solidified their dominance in a flurry of church-building activity throughout the South.

At the same time, many Southern Baptist individuals, by 1950, were living in other regions of the nation, reflecting the increasing mobility of families in the age of the automobile and a growing trend of job transfers. Businessman and professionals migrating from the Southeast's urban cities to northern and western coastal urban centers included an increasing number of Baptists. Many Baptists were also among the Texas and Oklahoma oil workers routinely transferred to refineries in Rocky Mountain states. The SBC in the 1940s abandoned prior commitments prohibiting infringement upon Northern/American

Baptist territory; in the 1950s, it wholeheartedly embraced western and northern expansion, rapidly entering into "pioneer" areas and establishing new congregations comprised primarily of transplanted Southerners. By the early 1960s, Southern Baptists could properly be described as a national denomination, albeit with a base heavily skewed to southern states.

Despite Southern Baptist successes, a long-awaited day of reckoning for the South and southern religion arrived on May 17, 1954, in the form of Brown v. Board of Education, the landmark Supreme Court decision declaring unconstitutional the long-standing practice of providing separate public school facilities for white and black children. Southern Baptist reaction was both swift and divergent, publicly exposing the growing disconnect between progressive national denominational leadership and culturally-conservative grassroots Southern Baptists. Days following the court decision, messengers to the annual SBC meeting passed a resolution (put forth by the denomination's Christian Life Commission) supporting the ruling, with some opposition. At the same time, state Baptist newspaper editors expressed views ranging from neutrality to open opposition, while letters to state Baptist papers largely voiced opposition and a number of congregations passed resolutions of protest.

> Southern Baptists comprised a large proportion of white Southerners who most vehemently opposed desegregation; many equated integration with socialism and a breach of the United States Constitution, in addition to being unbiblical and ungodly.

In the months and years following, opposition from Southern Baptists at the grassroots level contrasted noticeably with the pro-integration views of many national denominational leaders. Southern Baptists comprised a large proportion of white Southerners who most vehemently opposed desegregation;

many equated integration with socialism and a breach of the United States Constitution, in addition to being unbiblical and ungodly. In an effort to ensure that their children did not have contact with black children, many white Baptists initially called for the abolition of public schools, before settling upon a strategy of starting white-only "Christian" private schools. Others advocated and participated in violence against African Americans, including black Christians. Martin Luther King, Jr., was especially reviled by many white Baptists.

In short, Southern Baptists of the late 1950s confronted the racist heritage upon which their denomination had been founded, an ideology of white superiority and supremacy unvanquished by the Civil War and the century following. While many Southern Baptist leaders realized that the historical Baptist commitment to freedom stood in opposition to racism inherent in southern culture, their constituency by and large, having absorbed and reinforced southern white culture for generations, seemed unable or unwilling to embrace a freedom that transcended race. Roger Williams's seventeenth-century example of treating Native Americans as equals and Virginian John Leland's late-eighteenth-century advocacy of emancipation, it seemed, were forgotten; freedom existed only in the spiritual realm, as Leland in his later life and antebellum and Civil War-era Southern Baptists maintained. In what became known as the civil rights era, many Southern Baptists insisted that blacks could never be considered equals and should be prohibited from intermingling with whites at all costs.

The civil rights movement so consumed Southern Baptists that concurrent developments were quickly overshadowed by or entangled within or alongside the racial narrative. Westward expansion continued, but remained a secondary story line as only a handful of pioneer congregations emerged. The overall rate of Southern Baptist church and membership growth peaked in the 1950s and began sliding, never to recover, during the opening years of the civil rights struggle. At the same time, city congregations transitioned into an era of modern professionalism as congregations with seminary-trained ministers and support staff became the norm, even as many of these same churches refused to seat blacks in their sanctuaries.

Within the centrifuge of racial feelings and emotions forced to the surface by Brown v. Board of Education, two overarching and opposing narratives took shape. On the one side, a progressive mindset embraced the historical Baptist commitment to freedom of conscience and human equality, expressed in twentieth-century paradigms of academic freedom and racial inclusion (at least in theory); on the other, a fundamentalist-influenced worldview defended antebellum-era literal scriptural interpretation and southern racial segregation. Central to these divergent understandings stood the issue of education. Whereas more highly-educated Southern Baptists tended to fuse traditional Baptist principles with progressive thought, many less-educated persons were receptive to the theologically-reactionary, southern conservative framework.

Not surprisingly, Southern Baptist seminaries became a denominational focal point of theological and racial angst. Reflecting the theologically progressive bent of Southern Baptist leadership, the seminaries in the late 1950s came under increasing criticism from some conservatives. Midwestern Baptist Theological Seminary in Kansas City, the newest Southern Baptist seminary and the first located in the West, birthed in 1957 in the midst of racial upheaval and theological tension, quickly became a watershed flashpoint for Southern Baptists. In 1961, the BSSB's Broadman Press published Midwestern professor Ralph Elliott's book, *The Message of Genesis*. Elliott advocated the non-literal interpretation of the book of Genesis commonplace in Christian higher education, but one at odds with some conservative Southern Baptists. His opponents, a vocal minority of theologically fundamentalist southern preachers, succeeded in agitating for his removal from Midwestern Seminary.

The Elliott episode underscored a second wave of fundamentalism welling up in Southern Baptist life. Convention leadership responded in a fashion similar to the past by crafting a second statement of faith, the Baptist Faith and Message 1963, in effect a revision of the 1925 version, and intended to again mollify the convention's right wing. The 1963 rewrite followed the earlier statement by affirming basic doctrinal beliefs widely shared by Southern Baptists, disclaiming inappropriate authority in Southern Baptist life, and framing the wording in such a way as to accommodate all views from progressive to fundamentalist. As in 1925, the defensive action appeared to blunt the criticisms of fundamentalists. Yet, unlike the first time around, the fundamentalist agitators remained within the SBC, determined to extend their influence rather than to walk away as before.

Meanwhile, the volatile issue of race strained remaining vestiges of Southern Baptist harmony. From 1960 onward, Foy Valentine (1922-2006), head of the convention's Christian Life Commission, led the way among national leaders in advocating for civil rights, while many other progressive leaders maintained public neutrality. Annual convention attendees, typically seminary-educated and progressive preachers of fairly large, city congregations, provided some moderation to widespread grassroots opposition to segregation. Yet, the southern doctrine of white supremacy woven throughout the fabric of white southern religion remained a bond difficult to break. In the midst of the racial tension, the oldest Southern Baptist seminary became a denomination-wide test case when on April 19, 1961, Martin Luther King, Jr., spoke in chapel at the Southern Baptist Theological Seminary and received a standing ovation.

Within days, Southern Baptists widely condemned Southern Seminary's affirmation of King's message of racial equality. Dozens of Alabama churches voted to withhold financial contributions to the seminary. Letters to the editors of state papers expressed shock and outrage, and seminary trustees and President Duke K. McCall felt the need to issue a public apology for allowing King to speak at the seminary. Valentine and the Christian Life Commission notwithstanding, the seminary's recanting and progressive pastors' subsequent backpedaling to neutrality marked a formal retreat from civil rights advocacy. Southern Baptists, it seemed, could not be separated from their racist southern heritage.

Some Baptists, however, refused to stand down to grassroots racially-fueled opposition to freedom of conscience and human equality. Clarence Jordan (1912-1969), born in south Georgia, grew up witnessing the economic inequalities and racial tensions that characterized the American South. Called to the ministry, Jordan attended Southern Seminary in the 1930s, earning B.D. and Th.D. degrees while pastoring rural congregations in Kentucky. Convinced that the gospel called for racial harmony, he forsook the pastorate, turned down professorship offers, and moved with his wife, Florence, and four children back to rural Georgia. There he established Koinonia Farms, a biracial Christian community where blacks and whites lived and worked alongside one another, sharing meals and pooling the income from their crops. Ostracized, ridiculed, and threatened with death, Jordan persevered as a radical advocate for racial equality long before the civil rights movement, his Baptist faith guiding and sustaining his prophetic witness.

A graduate of Wake Forest College and Yale University, Baptist author and activist Will Campbell served first as a pastor and then as religious life director at the University of Mississippi in the early 1950s. He resigned from the latter in 1956 following death threats due to his support of integration. While involved with desegregation efforts, a stint with the National Council of Churches from 1957 to 1963, in turn, soured Campbell over the political correctness of the liberal organization, which did not appreciate his religious approach to social equality and did not understand his views on the humanity of his racist opponents.

Shaking off the restrictions of traditional organizations, Campbell struck out on his own, in 1964 forming the loosely-organized Committee of Southern Churchmen as a means of accomplishing his personal quest for racial reconciliation. Initially supported by a handful of Baptist professors and ministers and a sprinkling of non-Baptists (including Catholic writer Walker Percy and Trappist monk Thomas Merton), Campbell began his lifelong role as an independent Baptist agitator for social justice and peace.

A younger contemporary of Jordan and Campbell, and like Campbell born in Mississippi, historian Wayne Flynt turned from a planned career in ministry because of Southern Baptist opposition to integration. The violence of civil rights opponents during his young adult years influenced his life course as an advocate for civil rights, social justice, and economic uplift, an activism lived alongside an academic career, primarily as professor of history at Auburn University and author of numerous critically-acclaimed southern history volumes. Like Jordan and Campbell, Flynt lived and championed the Baptist witness for freedom of conscience apart from denominational office or church pulpit. Collectively, these three individuals represented the outer edges of progressivism among white Baptists in the South, as did other individuals such as ethics professors T. B. Maston at Southwestern Seminary and

Henlee Barnette at Southern Seminary.

Nonetheless, among Baptists, African Americans bore the burdens of a region's inhumanness and by their suffering moved Baptists forward yet again in the denomination's ongoing quest for freedom. For a number of decades, black Baptists focused on internal advancement. In 1925, the National Baptist Convention USA opened new building facilities for a publishing board, and during the next two decades, the NBC-USA focused its attention on lay training and paying down convention debt. Meanwhile, the fundamentalist/moderate theological battles experienced by white Baptists never materialized in African American Baptist life. Rather, the civil rights struggles of the 1950s framed the defining moments of black Baptist life of the twentieth century.

While Southern Baptists quickly engaged in divergent manners with the 1954 Brown v. Board of Education Supreme Court ruling, National Baptists instigated a policy of official detachment in response to disagreement among members. Although the NBC-USA in the late fifties did offer support for some of Martin Luther King's programs and methods, President Joseph H. Jackson (1905-1990) eschewed civil disobedience in favor of law and order. Many African American Baptists, however, insisted that the convention should more fully embrace the growing civil rights movement.

The tension between the strategies of civil disobedience and law and order came to a head in 1961 when King supported the nomination of Gardner C. Taylor, popular preacher and advocate for civil disobedience, for the NBC-USA presidency. When King's efforts failed, thirty-three delegates from fourteen states convened at Mount Zion Baptist Church in Cincinnati, Ohio, and formed a new organization, the Progressive National Baptist Convention (PNBC). Embracing religious activism, the PNBC, spiritual home to King and many other civil rights leaders, stood at the forefront of the civil rights movement of the 1960s; it endorsed the National Association for the Advancement of Colored People and affirmative action.

In 1963, the civil rights movement arrived at a pivotal juncture, and the support of the PNBC proved critical. In April, PNBC pastors King and Ralph Abernathy (1926-1990) sat in a Birmingham, Alabama, jail for demonstrating without a permit. Their arrest took place in the midst of a campaign to defy segregationist laws through non-violent means and force negotiations with local government leaders. From his cell, King read a letter from white clergy (including a fellow Baptist pastor, Earl Stalling of First Baptist, Birmingham) calling upon him and his allies to cease the demonstrations in the name of unity. Disappointed that white Christian leaders could not see the moral justice of the civil rights movement, King composed his now-famous "Letter from Birmingham Jail," in which he argued that civil rights would not be achieved without forceful but peaceful direct actions, declaring a "moral responsibility" for disobeying "unjust laws."

King's Birmingham jail letter became a rallying cry at a low point in the civil rights movement. Echoing the legacy of Baptist freedom fighters Roger Williams, Isaac Backus, and John Leland, all three of whom had petitioned government officials for repeal of discriminatory laws against religious non-conformists, King's letter placed African American Baptists front and center in the ongoing fight for human freedom and equality. The opposition included most white Baptists in the South, whose anger toward King's plea for freedom contributed to the September 15, 1963, terrorist bombing of the Sixteenth Street Baptist Church in Birmingham, an African American congregation. Four young girls were killed in the

> King's Birmingham jail letter became a rallying cry at a low point in the civil rights movement. Echoing the legacy of Baptist freedom fighters Roger Williams, Isaac Backus, and John Leland, all three of whom had petitioned government officials for repeal of discriminatory laws against religious non-conformists, King's letter placed African American Baptists front and center in the ongoing fight for human freedom and equality.

blast, while two more African American youth died in the melee that ensued.

Thus, 1963 drew to a close with Baptists locked in a larger struggle over the most pressing issues of human freedom and equality in America since the seventeenth- and eighteenth-century campaigns for religious liberty and the divisions over slavery and the Civil War. As in the Civil War, Baptists stood on both sides of the conflict, each claiming the mantle of freedom fighter. White Southern Baptists, with some notable exceptions, argued that freedom should be confined to the spiritual realm, while many white American Baptists embraced equal rights for blacks. Meanwhile, African American Baptists, advocating for civil rights, disagreed about the methods necessary to achieve the objectives. In the former Confederate states, power remained in the hands of white Southerners, although by the end of the year outrage over the Sixteenth Street Baptist Church bombing swung the momentum toward the non-violent, activist freedom voice of Progressive National Baptists King and Abernathy.

Meanwhile, fundamentalist Baptist groups, following decades of splintering, name-changing, and self-imposed separation from society and culture, rode the rising tide of a reactionary, conservative backlash against theological liberalism perceived among Southern and American Baptists and cultural liberalism at large. Their unapologetic conservatism, resulting in growing churches and institutions, translated into unprecedented influence. First Baptist Church of Hammond, Indiana, illustrated the ascendancy of fundamentalists. In 1959, the American Baptist-affiliated congregation of 700 members called as pastor Jack Hyles (1926-2001), a Southern Baptist-educated pastor-turned-fundamentalist. Assuming the pulpit, Hyles's style immediately drove several hundred members away; yet, within four years he built the congregation into one of the nation's first mega-churches, claiming over 2,000 members (it later became the nation's largest church in terms of weekly attendance). Hyles and Hammond Baptist in subsequent years founded six schools and a religious press, while Hyles authored forty-nine self-published books on theology that achieved a circulation of over 14 million copies.

Finally, yet another event in 1963 proved to be a pivotal development in a new narrative of a diverging commitment to freedom and the imperilment of the historic Baptist foundation of religious liberty and separation of church and state. The century thus far had witnessed a somewhat mixed record in the Baptist commitment to religious liberty, as ardent opposition to Roman Catholicism, spurred by the late-nineteenth-century Landmark movement and general Protestant distrust of Catholics, led to public Baptist campaigns against the Catholic Church and United States presidential candidates Albert Smith (1928) and John F. Kennedy (1960).

On a more positive note, the SBC in 1936 created the Committee on Public Relations to monitor religious liberty issues, followed one year later by the NBC's formation of a similar entity. Then, in an unprecedented display of post-antebellum cooperation between Baptists North and South, and black and white, the nation's two largest white Baptist groups (Northern and Southern Baptists) and largest black Baptist group (National Baptist Convention USA) in 1939 stood shoulder to shoulder in advocating religious liberty as expressed in their joint adoption of the American Baptist Bill of Rights. The three conventions and other Baptist bodies soon formalized the joint venture and in 1946 created the Washington, D.C.-based Joint Conference Committee on Public Relations. Under the leadership of Joseph M. Dawson, the Committee began publication of *Report from the Capital,* a periodical focused on the intersection of politics and faith. Renamed the Baptist Joint Committee on Public Affairs (BJCPA) in 1950, the organization, in the long-standing Baptist tradition of religious liberty and separation of church and state, supported the 1963 Supreme Court ruling Abington School District v. Schempp, a decision declaring mandatory Bible reading and prayer in public schools to be unconstitutional.

The 1963 court ruling was the fifth in a series of Supreme Court decisions addressing major religious liberty questions. In a prior fourteen-year time span, the Supreme Court had ruled that religious instruction in public schools violated the First Amendment's establishment clause (1948), that government could not censure a motion picture deemed offensive to religious beliefs (1952), that the state of Maryland could not require applicants for public office to swear belief in the existence of God (1961), and that public school prayers composed by government employees violated the First Amendment restriction against government sponsorship of prayer (1962). In short, from 1948 to 1963, the Supreme Court strongly defended the separation of church and state.

At the same time, the fear-laced decade of the 1950s witnessed a sudden public desire for civil expressions of faith. In the minds of many, America stood as a beacon of righteousness in a world threatened by godless communism. Brooks Hays (1898-1981), a longtime Democratic congressman and Baptist layman, as well as SBC president in 1957-1959, played a role in reviving civil religion. In 1953, one year after the formation of the National Day of Prayer, he sponsored a resolution to create a prayer room within the Capitol Building. Other political mandates followed, including the inclusion of the words "under God" to the American pledge of allegiance (1954), and the addition of the phrase "In God We Trust" to America's national motto (1956) and onto U.S. currency (1957). Pointing in opposite directions, the Supreme Court rulings and citizen-fueled congressional civil religion mandates hinted at imminent battles over the issue of separation of church and state, a conflict in which Baptists would play center stage.

FIVE

FREEDOM DEFENDERS

1964-2010

The dawning of 1964 evidenced a much-changed Baptist landscape worldwide from prior decades. This year included extraordinary developments in Baptist life globally and within the United States.

WESTERN DISSENT AND GLOBAL VITALITY

On New Year's Day, hosted by the Christian Study Center on Chinese Religions and Culture located atop a mountain called Tao Fung Shan outside of Hong Kong, fifty-nine Baptist leaders from throughout the world, the majority nationals and twelve American missionaries, assembled in a consultation on world missions. Representing national conventions related to the American Baptist Foreign Mission Society, Indian, Philippine, Thai, Japanese, Congolese, European, and American Baptists discussed church growth, evangelism, theology, ecumenism, and leadership development in a quest to frame a new vision for Baptist work worldwide. The Hong Kong meeting followed on the heels of the creation of the Baptist World Alliance Committee on Evangelism and Missions, a systematic effort to examine the current status of Baptists worldwide and develop a plan for future indigenous evangelism.

Meanwhile, the Brazilian Baptist Convention, most recent host of the BWA World Congress, was busy planning the launch of the region's first indigenous Baptist mass media blitz through the soon-to-be convention-owned Radio and Television Commission. At the same time, in Africa, Nigerian Baptist pastor James T. Ayorinde, former BWA vice-president, bore the distinction of being the first Nigerian leader of the rapidly-growing Nigerian Baptist Convention. In short, from Asia to Latin America to Africa, the ascendancy of Baptists in the Southern Hemisphere rapidly unfolded, a shifting landscape heralding a new chapter in the worldwide Baptist story.

Baptists in America, however, while yet committed to missions worldwide, wrestled with domestic issues of race and civil religion. Grassroots Southern Baptist resistance to integration contrasted with the growing, public morality of the civil rights movement. At the same time, as independent Baptist pastor Jerry Falwell proclaimed detachment from the civil rights movement (insisting that preachers were called to be soul winners, not politicians), separatist fundamentalists at large weighed engagement with culture in light of ascendant, populist civil religion and recent Supreme Court rulings regarding school prayer. Meanwhile, popular Baptist evangelist Billy Graham publicly embraced integration and distanced himself from his fundamentalist heritage, all the while positioning himself as a confidant of United States presidents. Within the swirling cauldron of racial battles and civil religion, cultural battle lines took shape, and the Baptist heritage of freedom and equality was caught in the middle.

In addition, American Baptist emphasis on social ministries and Southern Baptist Convention efforts to include, but pacify, fundamentalists portended the theological battle lines for the remainder of the twentieth century and into the twenty-first century. At the same time, a new age of financially-prosperous, professional, and multi-staffed local congregations in Southern Baptist life provided the early foundation for a then-unthinkable future development: the abandonment of denominational loyalties fostered so carefully since the foundation of the Cooperative Program in 1925.

In 1964, two specific events solidified cultural and theological divisions among Baptists in America, and the impact would last into the twenty-first century. The first occurred in the sanctuary of Watts Street Baptist Church in Durham, North Carolina. On April 9, Addie Davis (1917-2005), a student at Southeastern Baptist Theological Seminary, became the first woman pastor ordained in a Southern Baptist church. While ordination of women pastors had been taking place in Northern/American Baptist church life for decades, Davis's ordination further angered fundamentalists already at odds with SBC leadership over perceived cultural and theological liberalism within convention seminaries and agencies. The recipient of dozens of hate letters from fellow Baptists, Davis eventually was forced to leave Southern Baptist life and move northward to find congregational employment. Decades later, the successful fundamentalist effort to take control of the SBC hinged to no small degree on staunch opposition to women as church leaders, while the emergence of the alternative southern-centric Cooperative Baptist Fellowship (CBF) provided for some women long-sought opportunities to serve in congregational pastoral capacities.

The second and much more visible event in 1964 was the July 2 enactment of the U.S. Civil Rights Act, outlawing racial segregation in public life in America. In response, Falwell, dropping any pretenses of political disengagement, accused Martin Luther King, Jr., of being a left-wing communist, blamed the civil rights movement on communism and liberalism, and declared that America was imperiled morally. Falwell's narrative echoed views of Barry Goldwater-Republicans and provided the initial ideological framework for the formal emergence of the Religious Right in 1979. A parallel and related response in the form of an orchestrated fundamentalist takeover of the SBC also began in 1979.

The Civil Rights Act elevated the influence and prestige of leading African American Baptist pastors, in turn ushering in a new era of uplift focused on expansion of civil and political rights for minorities and rapid growth of black congregations. In addition, the U.S. Immigration and Nationality Act of 1965, by lifting non-European immigration quotas, contributed to broad, long-term ethnic changes that diminished the political power and cultural dominance of Caucasians at large and white Protestants in particular. As a result, Falwell's "Moral Majority" of the 1980s and 1990s, while providing a base for increasingly conservative Republican ideology, ultimately failed to shore up the defensive bulwark of white conservative Protestantism in the face of the incoming ethnic tide that propelled—with the overwhelming support of black Baptists—African American Barack Obama to the nation's presidency in 2008.

> In America, the fundamentalist redirection of the SBC, empowered by activist cultural conservatism and baptized by the rhetoric of biblical inerrancy, took practical shape in an unprecedented organizational crackdown against the historic Baptist principle of freedom of conscience.

Among Baptists at large, the events of the 1960s, both in America and beyond, provided the groundwork for radical internal changes by the end of the century. In America, the fundamentalist redirection of the SBC, empowered by activist cultural conservatism and baptized by the rhetoric of biblical inerrancy, took practical shape in an unprecedented organizational crackdown against the historic Baptist principle of freedom of conscience. The new fundamentalist denominational leaders, insistent that corporate doctrinal purity and theological correctness trumped individual freedom of conscience, transitioned the SBC from a confessional to a creedal stance, formally enacted in the passage of the 2000 Baptist Faith and Message as "an instrument of doctrinal accountability" for Southern Baptists.

While the quest for doctrinal purity led the convention into creedalism and statistical decline (baptisms and congregational support for the Cooperative Program dropped dramatically, for instance), a corresponding development in the 1980s and 1990s took the shape of a renewed Baptist commitment to freedom from traditional Baptist quarters. In some instances, the renewal transformed existing organizations. For example, the Baptist Joint Committee on Public Affairs—defunded in 1990 by a Southern Baptist Convention no longer fully appreciative of separation of church and state—was forced to rely more heavily upon other member Baptist groups for its very survival. Yet, within the two decades following, the BJC emerged in a stronger and more central position in Baptist life, and assumed a new title: Baptist Joint Committee for Religious Liberty.

The denominational renewal also found expression in the formation of new entities, including the Alliance of Baptists and CBF (denominational-like, missions-oriented organizations), Associated Baptist Press and Baptists Today (independent news organizations), Baptist Women in Ministry, Baptist History and Heritage Society (independent successor of the Southern Baptist Historical Society), a host of new moderate seminaries and divinity schools from Texas to Virginia, and the Baptist Center for Ethics and Christian Ethics Today Foundation.

Diverse in theology and ideology, CBF, birthed in 1990, evolved into the hub of "moderate Baptist" life and found expression in regional and state organizations, in addition to the national body headquartered in Atlanta. A missions and ministry-funding organization that partnered with other moderate Baptist entities committed to the common theme of freedom of conscience, CBF remained heavily southern-based. Nonetheless, in the early twenty-first century, CBF counted some congregations in California, Montana, New England, and points in-between. In addition, several traditional Southern Baptist-affiliated state conventions, including the Baptist General Association of Virginia and the Baptist General Convention of Texas, joined alongside CBF and other moderate organizations.

Collectively, these moderate Baptist organizations and others, their initial leadership comprised of former Southern Baptist leaders forced out of the SBC after unsuccessful attempts to stave off fundamentalists, represented a loosely-focused pushback against the new, ultraconservative SBC that reflected the political ideology of Falwell (formally aligned with Southern Baptists by the 1990s); the Calvinist, inerrantist theology of Albert Mohler (president of the Southern Baptist Theological Seminary); the cultural morality of Richard Land (director of the SBC Ethics and Religious Liberty Commission); and the historical revisionism represented by James Hefley (1931-2004, conservative apologist of the SBC takeover), David Barton (self-proclaimed historian and leading advocate of the myth of America's founding as a Christian nation), and Gregory Wills (Southern Seminary professor and author of a hagiographical history of the seminary, *Southern Baptist Theological Seminary, 1859-2009*).

As Southern Baptists, former Southern Baptists, and Cooperative Baptists of the late twentieth- and early twenty-first centuries faced-off over issues of freedom and conformity, American Baptists slowly descended into a theological and cultural freedom struggle of their own. While acceptance of the equality of women in ministry stirred little opposition among conservatives in American Baptist life, a movement by some congregations at the turn of the century to welcome homosexuals as church members and leaders led to regional divisions. Meanwhile, even as American Baptists of the early twenty-first century marketed the denomination as the nation's most racially-inclusive Baptist organization, stagnant membership and financial troubles plagued the denomination.

Among largely white Baptist denominations, the various coalitions of independent fundamentalist Baptists, now proudly wearing the badges of "cultural warriors," "religious right," and "evangelical," fared the best in the late twentieth and early twenty-first centuries. In addition to welcoming the transformation of the SBC into their ideological mold, independent fundamentalist Baptists benefited from a number of parallel developments. For instance, the growing popularity of ideologically-kindred para-church organizations, such as Campus Crusade for Christ and Focus on the Family, further buttressed ultra-conservative theological trends. In addition, the late-twentieth-century birth of the "Creationism" movement, a systematic and self-declared 1960s alternative scientific defense of a literal interpretation of the Genesis creation account, provided a new weapon in the fight against perceived liberalism. Creationism subsequently morphed into "scientific creationism" in the 1980s and "intelligent design" in the first decade of the twenty-first century. Also, political alliances with the Republican Party, beginning with U.S. President Ronald Reagan, garnered yet more influence and public recognition for Falwell and Pat Robertson and their respective Baptist universities, Liberty and Regents.

Whereas in the early twentieth century, the fundamentalist masses were often dismissed as uneducated and poor, by the end of the century, the movement transcended socioeconomic boundaries. Beneath the umbrella of the Religious Right (whose base included many independent and Southern Baptist fundamentalists) evolved dozens of organized movements aimed at repealing separation of church and state and securing special judicial privileges for Christians, including the enactment of Old Testament morality into American law and jurisprudence. Vision America, led by Southern Baptist Rick Scarborough, represented one such organizational effort to transition the United States from democracy to theocracy. Other theocratic-leaning organizations with Baptist connections included Council on Biblical Manhood and Womanhood, Eagle Forum, Family Research Council, and Council for National Policy, the latter formed by Southern Baptist Tim LaHaye, author of the popular *Left Behind* book series.

On the other hand, disagreements existed among independent fundamentalists over matters of theology (such as Calvinism and Arminianism), culture (such as appropriate dress), and social engagement (such as views of secular entertainment). At the same time, some Southern Baptists never embraced

While fundamentalist Baptists represented a mostly white theological, cultural, and political backlash against perceived liberalism, African American Baptists of the late twentieth and early twenty-first centuries, empowered by civil rights victories of the 1960s and disinterested in fundamentalism, experienced unprecedented growth and achieved new influence within Baptist life at large.

fundamentalism, despite efforts by their leaders to enforce doctrinal purity. Many Southern Baptist churches loosened ties with the convention, while in the first decade of the twenty-first century rifts developed among convention leaders and other prominent individuals. In short, Southern Baptist leadership fractured along issues related to missionary requirements (prompted by policies prohibiting charismatic practices and narrowing baptism parameters), theological nuances (including Calvinism), generational themes (younger leaders' embracing of environmentalism, for example), financial problems (wasteful spending and budgetary declines), and leadership controversies (partially reflected in incompetent leaders and secretive meetings). Wade Burleson, pastor of Emmanuel Baptist Church in Enid, Oklahoma, and International Mission Board trustee from 2005 until his forced resignation in 2008, emerged as the informal leader of a growing backlash against the extreme fundamentalism of SBC leadership.

While fundamentalist Baptists represented a mostly white theological, cultural, and political backlash against perceived liberalism, African American Baptists of the late twentieth and early twenty-first centuries, empowered by civil rights victories of the 1960s and disinterested in fundamentalism, experienced unprecedented growth and achieved new influence within Baptist life at large. Emerging as the second largest Baptist group in America, the National

Baptist Convention, USA mirrored the organizational effectiveness of the SBC, replete with boards, agencies, and auxiliaries. Denominational involvement, however, exceeded that of Southern Baptists by 2010. Despite having approximately half the number of churched members as the SBC, and 30,000 congregations compared to the SBC's 45,000, attendances at general annual meetings typically exceeded those of Southern Baptists, while attendance at the Christian Educators Conference (of which there is no parallel in Southern Baptist life) attracted up to 50,000 or more annually, making the conference the largest annual meeting of any kind among Baptists in America.

Yet, institutional triumphs reveal only part of the story of black Baptists in America. Together black Baptists presented and lived out a gospel that fused personal faith, corporate social uplift, individual financial prosperity, and business acumen. During convention meetings, for example, new Cadillacs shared vendor floor space with financial institutions, book publishers, Sunday School literature, and missions advocacy organizations. Combined, the three black Baptist conventions in America—National Baptist Convention, USA, National Baptist Convention America, and Progressive National Baptist Convention—rivaled the SBC in size and scope by the early twenty-first century. In 2005, the three organizations began efforts to work more closely together, a development further encouraged by the 2008 emergence of the New Baptist Covenant, a loosely-formed coalition of some 20 million moderate Baptists of North America (of whom black Baptists represented the majority) united in affirming the common Baptist values of religious liberty, evangelism, and social ministries.

> Meanwhile, led by Hispanic Baptists, ethnic Baptists at large provided the greatest growth among Baptists in America in the closing decades of the twentieth century and the early twenty-first century.

Meanwhile, led by Hispanic Baptists, ethnic Baptists at large provided the greatest growth among Baptists in America in the closing decades of the twentieth century and the early twenty-first century. By the 1990s, the growing number of Hispanic Baptists allowed the SBC to temporarily maintain stability in its membership. Reflecting ethnic patterns in Texas at large, Hispanic Baptists in the Lone Star state more than tripled in numbers during the first decade of the twenty-first century. Rapid growth among Oklahoma and Nevada Baptists (and others) ensued, while the Baptist General Convention of Texas became the leading advocate of Hispanic ministry through theological education, church starts, and consultation with other state conventions. Asian Baptists experienced growth in California and other large American cities. Seattle, Washington, emerged as a melting pot of ethnic Baptist expressions. Native American Baptist work progressed slowly on Indian reservations in the Southwest, Montana, and the Dakotas.

Notwithstanding the prominence of Baptists in American religious life, however, the greater story of modern Baptists took place in the Southern Hemisphere. From 1990 to 2010, Baptists worldwide grew by roughly 50 percent, despite stagnation in North America. African Baptists experienced the greatest growth during this time, expanding at a rate of roughly 350 percent despite severe political, economic, and social problems among many African nations. Rapid growth also occurred in Latin America (and to a lesser extent in southern Asia and Australia) against the backdrop of rapidly expanding evangelicalism at large. While trending more to charismatic influences than in America or Europe, Southern Hemisphere Baptists also advocated a more holistic ministry than many of their counterparts elsewhere and exhibited heightened concerns for poverty, hunger, religious liberty, and HIV/AIDS, while largely rejecting Western religious fundamentalism and capitalistic Christianity.

Whereas American and European missionaries of the past had largely shaped Baptist expressions in other lands, Western missionary organizations of the late twentieth and twenty-first centuries more typically assumed support roles of enabling nationals rather than directing Baptist work. Meanwhile, international evangelicals increasingly sent missionaries to America, particularly to poverty-ridden inner city populations of the United States, metropolitan areas largely forsaken by suburban-trending American congregations. CBF, recognizing the borderless nature of the new global age, structured their missions agency as "Global Missions" focused on people groups rather than geographical boundaries. In addition to mission work among displaced and underserved people groups (including Gypsies and Native Americans), CBF appointed David and Ana D'Amico (1936-2009) as missionaries to the United Nations in order to spread the Baptist witness, promote human rights, advance ecumenical opportunities, and foster relationships among diplomats worldwide.

African American Baptist international mission efforts, in turn, focused primarily on mission partnerships with African nations and communities, emphasizing health, education, and ministry. Like Cooperative Baptists, their mission efforts took place in the context of partnership with the Baptist World Alliance.

Southern Baptist leaders, however, took an opposite tact: unhappy with perceived theological impurity among many international Baptists and suspicious of social ministries, the SBC in 2004 pulled out of the global Baptist family represented by the BWA. Yet, instead of weakening the BWA, the departure of fundamentalist critics ushered the worldwide organization of Baptists into an era of renewed strength and vitality. Under the leadership of General Secretary Neville Callam, a Jamaican Baptist, some 215 of approximately 250 Baptist groups worldwide were affiliated with the BWA by 2010, working together to advance the Baptist witness as expressed in evangelism, religious liberty, human rights, education, and social advocacy.

Finally, the tilting of the Baptist witness to the Southern Hemisphere was reflected in a 2009 BWA statistics report. Africa had over 31,000 Baptist congregations with 7.5 million members; Asia, over 29,000 churches and 5.3 million congregants; and Central and South America, over 15,000 churches and 2 million members. Europe, meanwhile, had 12,500 congregations with 765,000 members. Southern hemispheric nations claiming over one million Baptists each included Brazil, the Democratic Republic of Congo, Myanmar, and Nigeria. In short, by the end of the first decade of the twenty-first century, the BWA in partnership with Baptist groups apart from Europe and North America achieved numerical and organizational strength, and assumed ministries of a greater diversity and scope, than their Western counterparts.

INSTITUTIONAL TRANSFORMATION
AN EVOLUTION OF INFLUENCE IN SOUTHERN
BAPTIST AND INDEPENDENT BAPTIST LIFE

Prior to the arrival of cheap, mass transportation enabled by the automobile in the early twentieth century, local congregations stood at the center of Baptist life. While the story of the nineteenth century included the founding and rapid growth of a myriad of regional and national Baptist organizations, the number of Baptists actively participating in such organizations—pastors who attended the meetings, missionaries funded by missionary agencies, leaders elected or appointed, advocacy-oriented laypersons, and employees on organizational payrolls—remained small. Simply stated, the cost of denominational involvement, whether measured in terms of travel restrictions, educational attainment, personal interest, or time availability, remained prohibitive for a worldwide community of faith comprised largely of uneducated, rural farming families, and the urban poor.

To illustrate, the 293 delegates to the 1845 formative meeting of the SBC held at the First Baptist Church in Augusta, Georgia, consisted almost entirely of wealthy South Carolinians and Georgians, a small minority in Baptist life, who could reasonably afford the time and expense of traveling to Augusta by rail, horse, or buggy. In contrast, local church revivals and other special church events in towns large and small attracted common folk and collectively garnered more routine mainstream media attention (albeit typically local coverage) than did periodic meetings of denominational organizations.

While nineteenth-century lack of easy accessibility to the workings of denominational organizations ensured that local congregations remained the primary public focus of Baptist life, the automobile brought about the democratization of denominationalism. At the same time, twentieth-century organizational methods and mass communication ensured higher visibility of denominational statements and actions, which, in turn, elicited responses, whether supportive or contentious, from individual congregations. In short, denominational organizations arguably assumed a greater role in the public shaping of Baptist identity than did the congregations they served, as Charles Spurgeon in the last decade of the nineteenth century discovered in British Baptist life. Despite unparalleled prominence among British Baptists, Spurgeon and the Metropolitan Tabernacle proved powerless to prevent theological and organizational change within the Baptist Union.

Yet, if Spurgeon had made his stand in the mid-twentieth century, the outcome may have been different, thanks to modern communication technologies that quickly birthed a new challenger to denominational organizations as shapers of Baptist identity: individual Baptist giants sitting in front of radio microphones and, later, television cameras. In the United States, the modern media revolution enabled a relative handful of publicly-visible individuals to become stand-ins for grassroots independent, fundamentalist Baptists and challengers to captains of denominational agencies.

William Riley, Frank Norris, Bob Jones, and Jerry Falwell, for example, successively emerged as popular independent voices of fundamentalist Baptists in America by delivering their sermons, speeches, and diatribes against liberalism to large audiences via radio and, later, television. During the same time, in Southern Baptist life Edgar Mullins, George Truett, Foy Valentine, and Duke McCall served as notable SBC leaders. In the matchup between independent, dogmatic media personalities and Southern Baptist officials, the common folk fervency inspired by the former stood in contrast to the loyal but low-key following garnered by the scholarly accolades, professional achievements, and denominational status of the latter.

Establishment leaders realized the times were changing, and tried to contain rising populist sentiment. In 1926, the year following the SBC's endorsement of the Baptist Faith and Message, fundamentalists proved helpless to counter the organizational edict, and soon largely withdrew from Southern Baptist life. However, in the years following the 1963 passage of the revised Baptist Faith and Message, denominational leadership, acknowledging resurgent fundamentalism, further sought to placate their ideological opponents by welcoming the election of popular conservative Wally A. Criswell (1909-2002, pastor of First Baptist Church of Dallas, Texas) to the convention presidency (1969-1971).

The strategic move worked, but only temporarily. Marveling at the taste of denominational politics and desiring more power, yet still held at organizational arms-length, Southern Baptist fundamentalists reassessed the SBC landscape. Forward-thinking fundamentalists realized they held a winning hand. The key resided in the systematic marriage of culturally-conservative populism to theological conservatism, delivered through the media of television and radio, alongside printed literature, into the homes of white Baptists shaken by civil rights unrest, communist threats, and Supreme Court rulings limiting expressions of civil religion. Preying upon the fear generated by such cultural changes, they set about recruiting foot soldiers from pulpit and pew.

At the same time, traditional Baptists, by now highly vested in the SBC as a denomination, failed to fully recognize the power of new media. The media disconnect between fundamentalists and traditional Baptists found expression in surprising ways. In general, fundamentalist Baptists embraced new technologies and media formats as effective tools for delivering an anti-liberal message to the Baptist public. Following a brief period of resistance in the 1960s, for example, they embraced a new generation of Christian musicians who wedded evangelical theology to contemporary, and popular, musical styles. Meanwhile, Southern Baptist denominational leaders, despite the 1941 establishment of the Radio Commission, continued to focus on denominational institutions as shapers of public Baptist perception. The convention's long-running radio program, The Baptist Hour, however, never attracted the grassroots enthusiasm or widespread airplay as that garnered by numerous fundamentalist Baptist personalities. Likewise, moderate to conservative Baptists, committed to traditional worship styles, made little effort to adapt to popular musical tastes. Fundamentalists, in short, used contemporary cultural media to oppose theological and cultural progressivism, while traditionalists proved more receptive to theological and cultural progressivism but resistant to new cultural media.

As a result, by the late 1970s, household Baptist names included evangelist Billy Graham and fundamentalists Falwell, Criswell, Charles Stanley (pastor of First Baptist Church, Atlanta), and Adrian Rogers (1931-2005, pastor of Bellevue Baptist Church in Cordova, Tennessee), men whose popularity resulted directly from widespread radio and television exposure. In contrast, no Southern Baptist officials, seminary presidents, or agency heads gained comparable widespread following among grassroots Baptists. Unbeknownst to most Southern Baptist leaders, a revolution was brewing.

Amassing and instructing a loyal support base, fundamentalist strategists, in turn, implemented a systematic, political takeover of SBC machinery through the ballot box at annual meetings, over the course of two decades gradually purging all traditional Baptists—considered liberals by fundamentalists—from denominational boards and agencies. The SBC as an organization, in short, experienced radical transformation by a modern media-centric strategy that galvanized previously uninvolved, minority fundamentalists in a successful political quest to capture denominational seats of power. Despite long-standing institutional advantages, traditional Baptists exhibited neither the political will nor marketing savvy to effectively counter the ultraconservative incumbents.

CONGREGATIONAL LIFE
REVISIONING ACTIVISM, SEPARATISM, GENDER, AND GEOGRAPHY AMONG BAPTISTS WORLDWIDE

Since the seventeenth century, local Baptist communities of faith have provided fertile ground for a kaleidoscope of Baptist movements and expressions, from religious liberty activism to abolitionist agitation to theological nuances to civil rights campaigns and evangelistic and social ministry innovations. While among white Baptists in America the ascendancy of formal denominational structures in the nineteenth century and technology-enabled individual Baptist superstars in the twentieth century refocused some attention away from the local church, the influence of local congregations never ceased.

Remaining at the core of Baptist ecclesiology through the centuries, local church autonomy served to counter the overreaching of Baptist institutions; associations, conventions, agencies, and societies ultimately exercised no authority over any individual congregation. Baptist institutions thus thrived if supported by local churches, and struggled or even died without adequate congregational participation. The earliest Baptist associations of the eighteenth century were careful not to infringe upon local church autonomy, while national conventions and societies of the nineteenth century reflected the collective wishes of their constituent congregations and struggled to answer criticisms originating from within congregations. In America, for example, early anti-mission movements, Primitive Baptists, and Landmark expressions represented nineteenth-century local church-centric movements that opposed Baptist institutionalization and forced adjustments on the part of Baptist organizations. In nineteenth-century Europe, the widespread movement toward institutionalism likewise met resistance in some local church quarters. Nonetheless, denominationally-originated resources otherwise unavailable to local congregations ensured a generally mutually beneficial relationship between institution and congregation, especially in the Western world.

While nineteenth-century local church opposition to denominationalism failed to prevent Baptist institutionalism, it served to heighten the primacy of local church autonomy and proved fertile ground for Baptist activism (abolitionism, women's movements, and the Social Gospel, for example) that, in turn, reshaped institutionalism. In a similar fashion, failed fundamentalist opposition of the early twentieth-century reshaped both Northern and Southern Baptists, in both instances pushing denominational trajectories in more theologically liberal (Northern) and moderate (Southern) directions, while fundamentalists formed their own separatist organizations. In the meantime, growing denominational resources, not the least of which took the shape of Sunday School literature, cemented loyalty among many congregations.

During the late twentieth century, the civil rights movement in America illustrated the primacy that some local churches gave to fostering and shaping activism; whereas both white and black Baptist denominational institutions expressed caution and/or opposition to the movement, local black congregations provided the moral impetus and leadership to ensure enactment of civil rights. Decades later, many Baptist institutions in America and Canada took fervent stands against AIDS (the judgment of God on homosexuals) and homosexuality (the worst of sins), only to witness a growing congregational perception, fueled by some in a new generation of younger Baptists, of AIDS as a human tragedy and homosexuality as genetically-driven rather than a choice.

On a broader scale, Baptist congregations at the turn of the twenty-first century, other than fundamentalist churches at large, increasingly focused on meeting the needs of the poor in their communities and embracing environmentally-friendly initiatives. At the same time, fundamentalist congregational activism typically found expression in selective pro-life advocacy (vocal anti-abortion sentiment contrasted with pro-war and pro-death penalty beliefs, with little if any public concern for human rights and human welfare at large); insistence upon traditional gender and sexual norms (denying women the same rights as men and insisting that sexual activity be confined to married persons of the opposite gender); and a pro-wealth, pro-capitalist viewpoint (opposition to global warming and public health care on economic grounds, small government anti-tax advocacy, and anti-union sentiment). SBC denominational ethicist Richard Land, for example, argued that the civil institution of marriage should be subservient to fundamentalist biblical theology, while his allegiance to free market capitalism compelled him to equate public health care to Nazism.

Meanwhile, in Africa congregational Baptist activism focused on feeding the impoverished, providing basic health care, preventing untimely deaths, caring for AIDS victims, and human rights advocacy in general. Latin American Baptists generally echoed the same impulses, while Asian Baptist and Eastern European congregations, bearing the burden of a more widespread legacy of religious persecution, focused on religious liberty and human rights issues. Australian Baptist congregational activism, by way of contrast, tended to include a mixture of social progressivism and political conservatism. In short, against the backdrop of less-established institutionalization than that of Baptists in America and Western Europe, as well as in the context of impoverished nations and people groups, international Baptist churches often stood on the frontlines of a daily struggle between freedom and persecution and life and death.

Growing congregational activism, in turn, developed hand-in-hand with a corollary trend in America: congregational separatism. When Southern Baptist pastors Criswell, Stanley, and Rogers—three fundamentalists openly critical of the pre-fundamentalist SBC—emerged as household names in

Southern Baptist circles of the late twentieth century, their successes signaled a transition in the relationship between congregation and denomination. While the SBC depended upon the financial resources of local congregations to meet growing denominational ambitions—such as the 1976 launch of Bold Mission Thrust, a failed convention campaign to preach the gospel to all the world by the year 2000—the mega-church congregations of Criswell, Stanley, and Rogers, having established in-house ownership of missions and literature (two domains previously reserved to denomination entities), did not need institutional resources. The larger dynamics of this development indicated the re-ascendancy of the local congregation to a place of denominational independence in Baptist life, a pattern echoed across the globe from the eighties to the present against the backdrop of what is commonly referred to as a "post-denominational" era.

In short, post-denominational trends in twenty-first-century Christianity found expression in congregations' public disassociation from denominational entities, internal self-reliance, and a movement toward faith that downplayed denominational distinctives. Some post-denominationalist congregations oriented themselves along theological axes: evangelical or non-evangelical, fundamental or liberal, conservative or progressive. Others, loosely grouped as Emerging or Emergent congregations, sought to move beyond theological and political barriers in order to arrive at a core of the Christian faith that transcended contemporary church traditions yet was interwoven in church history, rooted in the teachings of Christ, and resonant in the global age. While Baptists offered mixed reactions to the movement, the Emerging/Emergent church found enthusiastic reception among many younger, moderate Baptists in America and Western Europe.

In addition to congregational activism and separation, some local Baptist churches of the late twentieth and early twenty-first centuries increasingly included women in formal leadership roles. Both in America (other than among fundamentalists) and globally (with the exception of Muslim-centric and culturally-patriarchical nations), women in Baptist congregations, in the face of larger cultural and social currents empowering women, experienced more, but still limited, opportunities to move beyond traditional religious barriers and serve as deacons, preachers, and pastors. In addition, women's prominent roles in social and mission ministries expanded. For example, Baptist Women in Ministry, a national women's advocacy organization headquartered in Atlanta, focused on fostering women's leadership at the congregational level, primarily in the South.

Also, congregational activism, separatism, and gender inclusiveness expressed in much Baptist life of the late twentieth and early twenty-first centuries took place alongside a new understanding of the congregation as a "glocal church," that is, a local church with a global vision and mission connections. Baptist laity increasingly perceived themselves—their training, skills, and talents—as able to directly engage mission work in an ongoing manner within the context of local church mission teams in an era of easy access to global travel. Following the American development of the proliferation of church youth mission trips of the 1970s and 1980s, a growing number of local congregations placed value on "hands-on" missions, in turn leading to one-on-one partnerships with other congregations, both nationally and internationally. Mission activity increasingly took place outside of institutional mission boards and agencies, and a sharply decreasing percentage of congregational financial resources flowed into mission boards and agencies.

Congregational transformation, in summary, reflected the ongoing freedom narrative of Baptist life. To be certain, motives varied among contemporary Baptists. Many found inspiration in the foundational Baptist beliefs of individual freedom of conscience and local church autonomy. Others utilized the language of freedom but restricted its application to like-minded persons. Nonetheless, congregations of the late twentieth and early twenty-first centuries exercised a greater degree of self-freedom than in prior decades.

STATESMEN, SCHOLARS, PREACHERS, POLITICIANS, AND PROPHETS
NOTABLE BAPTIST INDIVIDUALS

While the story of recent Baptist history can be told from both denominational and congregational perspectives, it cannot be told apart from individual contributions. The Baptist commitment to a New Testament faith and to a grounding in the freedom of conscience ensures that the convictions of individual believers ultimately influence corporate expressions of Baptist community and sometimes serve as a check to unhealthy and unscriptural corporate trends and movements. In America and Europe, Baptists' religious liberty fight of the seventeenth and eighteenth centuries, slavery struggles of the nineteenth century, and the civil rights movement of the twentieth century were instances in which courageous individuals with strong personal, biblical convictions provided leadership from within the Baptist community that defined and redefined the larger Baptist identity.

The transformative contributions of a number of Baptist individuals of the modern American era have already been noted, such as Martin Luther King, Jr., Addie Davis, Foy Valentine, Billy Graham, Jerry Falwell, and W. A. Criswell. While no listing is exhaustive, the contributions of a handful of other Baptists, both in America and the world at large, merit mention as representatives of individuals who shaped Baptist life and thought in the most recent era.

Among Baptist statesmen in America of the late twentieth century, few likely labored harder with less national recognition than Herschell E. Daney, a tireless Native American and American Baptist leader who, in addition to serving as an ABC administrator and advocate for Native Americans, also served as missionary, pastor, and professor. More publicly visible was R. Keith Parks, longtime missionary and president of the SBC Foreign Mission Board from 1980 to 1992, and Global Missions Coordinator for the Cooperative Baptist Fellowship from 1993 to 1999. Under Parks's leadership, the SBC reached its peak of missions growth and expansion, and CBF established a new paradigm of missions without borders, reflective of modern global realities.

Few statesmen exercised as much far-reaching influence as Carolyn Weatherford Crumpler, who served on and visited many mission fields, in addition to leading Southern Baptists' Woman's Missionary Union and playing a key role in the formation and direction of CBF. Also bridging SBC and CBF life, Cecil Sherman, pastor, professor, and denominational leader, emerged from the SBC fundamentalist controversy of the 1980s as a leader among moderate Baptists, steering CBF in its formative years as coordinator (1992-1996). Daniel Vestal followed a similar route, serving as a prominent pastor prior to assuming a leadership role within CBF, culminating with his service as executive coordinator since 1996. The stories of Parks, Crumpler, Sherman, and Vestal provide a snapshot of a pre-fundamentalist SBC and encapsulate the story of how CBF sought to preserve Baptist freedoms from the throes of the SBC fundamentalist controversy by creating a denominational home for several thousand Baptist congregations.

Among African American Baptists, William J. Shaw emerged as one of the more influential statesmen of the current era, serving as pastor of White Rock Baptist Church in Philadelphia since 1956 and holding numerous denominational positions within the National Baptist Convention, USA, including the presidency since 1999. Within British Baptist life, David Coffey served as one of the most visible statesmen. Chosen as the general secretary of the Baptist Union of Great Britain in 1991, Coffey was elected as president of the Baptist World Alliance in 2005, serving the latter organization during a time of rapid growth and expansion.

A number of selected scholars also contributed significantly to recent Baptist life, including (in alphabetical order): David W. Bebbington (a Scottish Baptist, historian, and professor at the University of Stirling since 1976, Bebbington's work on British Baptists influenced contemporary views of Baptist history); Lincoln S. Brownell, Jr. (born in Monrovia, Liberia, Brownell received theological training in Africa and America and became the first Liberian to serve as president of Liberia Baptist Theological Seminary); E. Glenn Hinson (moderate Baptist and prominent professor of church history and spirituality for many decades); Lilian Lim (1959-2009, Asian Baptist theologian who in 2005 was named president of Asia Baptist Graduate Theological Seminary); Bill J. Leonard (moderate Baptist, longtime professor, world-renowned church historian, and leading interpreter of recent Baptist history); Leon McBeth (former professor at Southwestern Baptist Theological Seminary, author of the popular 1987 *The Baptist Heritage* college and seminary textbook); Molly T. Marshall (professor of theology and popular author who in 2004 became the first woman president of an accredited Baptist seminary, American Baptists' Central Baptist Theological Seminary in Kansas City, Kansas—now in Shawnee, Kansas); R. Albert Mohler (recognized as a leading scholar among fundamentalist and Calvinist Southern Baptists and president of Southern Baptist Theological Seminary); and Walter B. Shurden (moderate Baptist, former popular professor at Southern Seminary and Mercer University, and one of the most widely-read recent Baptist historians worldwide).

In short, the most prominent Baptist scholars of the late twentieth and early twenty-first centuries worked in the fields of history and theology. The most widely-respected historians were found within the ranks of traditional and moderate Baptists, while influential theologians represented the ideological spectrum of Baptist life. With the ascension and widespread establishment of fundamentalism in denominational Baptist life, scholarly struggles over historical interpretation and theological paradigms played a significant role in shaping a new generation of clergy and laity.

In effect, Southern Baptist seminaries of the early twenty-first century harbored fundamentalists and Calvinists, while recently-founded moderate Baptist theological schools (such as Baptist Theological Seminary of Richmond and McAfee School of Theology in Atlanta) anchored a broader theological and ideological spectrum. Absorbing a generation of outcast progressive Southern Baptist professors, the moderate institutions produced a new wave of historians who interpreted Baptists in a broader religious and social context, as well as theologians (dubbed "Bapto-Catholics") who drifted away from the historical Baptist position of individual freedom of conscience into hierarchical, sacramental religion. Baptist theological education trends worldwide reflected similar patterns, while outside of Baptist institutions some public university history and religion departments aided in the training of young, typically moderate, Baptist scholars.

While statesmen shaped denominations and scholars assisted in reshaping Baptist thought, prominent preachers and pastors of the late twentieth and early twenty-first centuries delivered various portraits of the gospel message from the pulpits of Baptist congregations. In America, Fred Shuttlesworth (pastor of churches in Birmingham and Cincinnati) and Gardner C. Taylor (pastor of Concord Baptist Church of Christ in Brooklyn, New York, for four decades), both leaders in the early civil rights struggles, remained influential black Baptist preachers for decades afterwards; Shuttlesworth was known for his ongoing advocacy for civil rights, and Taylor as one of the great sermon crafters of his era. Recognized orators among Southern Baptists included fundamentalist Charles Stanley, moderate Richard A. Jackson (former pastor of North Phoenix Baptist Church in Arizona), and Rick Warren, pastor of Saddleback Community Church in California, all three of whom pastored megachurch congregations, baptized tens of thousands, and authored numerous books. Also in America, John Piper, pastor of Bethlehem Baptist Church in Minneapolis, served as a leading pastoral spokesperson for Calvinist Baptists. Meanwhile, in Brazil, Ruben Lopez (1871-1979), pastor of Vila Mariana Baptist Church in Sao Paulo, impacted all of Latin America with his sermons, leading the BWA to enact large-scale

> In short, the most prominent Baptist scholars of the late twentieth and early twenty-first centuries worked in the fields of history and theology. The most widely-respected historians were found within the ranks of traditional and moderate Baptists, while influential theologians represented the ideological spectrum of Baptist life.

evangelism efforts throughout the region.

In addition, Baptists of this era were not without their share of American political figures, the most well-known of whom included: Jimmy Carter (Baptist laymen and Sunday School teacher at Maranatha Baptist Church in Plains, Georgia, and president of the United States from 1977 to 1981); William J. Clinton (Arkansas native and U.S. president from 1993 to 2001); and Albert Gore (a Tennessean and Clinton's vice-president and a later presidential candidate). Following the end of his political service, Carter became a leading moderate Baptist figurehead and spokesperson for unity among non-fundamentalist Baptists, Clinton served as an advocate for racial justice, and Gore found a welcome reception among moderate Baptists for his environmental message. All three were Democrats; fundamentalist and conservative Baptists widely condemned their perceived liberal policies and moderate theology.

On the other side of the political aisle were well-known Republicans such as senators Newt Gingrich of Georgia (formerly Baptist) and Jesse Helms (1921-2008) of North Carolina; presidential candidates John McCain of Arizona and Michael Huckabee of Arkansas, the latter a former Baptist minister and former governor of Arkansas; and Alabama Republican and state Chief Justice Roy Moore, whose placement of a Ten Commandments statue in the Alabama state courthouse created a nationwide furor in 2003 and 2004. All attracted a large degree of political support from fundamentalist and conservative Baptists.

Finally, traditional Baptists produced a number of prophetic voices during late-twentieth- and early-twenty-first-century America, such as Millard Fuller (1939-2009; founder of Habitat for Humanity and the Fuller Center for Housing, Fuller spearheaded Baptist and Christian activism for providing affordable housing for persons living in poverty); James Dunn (executive director of the Baptist Joint Committee in 1981-1999, and a leading voice for religious liberty and separation of church and state); Tony Campolo (American Baptist professor of sociology at Eastern College, popular and prolific author, and an outspoken advocacy for the Social Gospel); Sarah Frances Anders (sociologist at Louisiana College and advocate and analyst of Baptist women in ministry); and Bill Moyers (award-winning American journalist who explored themes of faith, politics, and life from a moderate Baptist perspective).

CONCLUSION

The Baptist story thus far has unfolded beneath a canopy of four centuries of freedom-centric witness, a paradigm more suited for a minority faith than for establishment religion. Now a major global faith anchored in the Southern Hemisphere, Baptists at the dawn of their fifth century nonetheless confront many of the same challenges that their faith forebears faced: freedom of conscience and religion are non-existent or tenuous in many locales, while theological, ecclesial, and institutional tensions yet remain.

The Baptist faith today is challenged by a rapidly-changing globe shrunk to the size of an Internet web browser while yet divided by ageless socioeconomic, religious, ethnic, and racial problems. Perhaps the most unexpected (and among the most vexing) of contemporary developments in Baptist life is the widespread denial among some Baptists in America of the historic Baptist support for separation of church and state. A reflection primarily of involvement with the politically-oriented Religious Right, church-state union is currently embraced by many western believers who oppose historic Baptist commitments championed by Baptist groups affiliated with the global Baptist World Alliance and the American-based Baptist Joint Committee for Religious Liberty.

The complexity of continuity and change indicate that Baptists are a fabric of movements, individuals, congregations, and institutions that, at times, has stretched the limits of its collective stitching. The Baptist story is broadly contained within the borders of voluntary faith, believer's baptism, local church autonomy, and a strong dependence on New Testament theology. Many Baptists today value the Baptist narrative as handed down from Thomas Helwys, Roger Williams, John Clarke, John Leland, and others. Individuals, movements, and institutions grounded in this narrative reflect a robust faith committed to religious liberty for all persons and separation of church and state, rooted in the sacredness of individual conscience, anchored in Christ, and expressed in a worldwide community of faith that welcomes Christian diversity and humanity at large. To faithful fifth-century Baptists falls the task of remembering, reaffirming, and expressing anew the Baptist heartbeat of freedom.

ENDNOTES

GENERAL

The narrative of Baptist history presented in this volume is a broad summary of historical consensus articulated by mainstream Baptist and religious historians of the late twentieth and early twenty-first centuries. It also represents the results of personal research in primary documents of the seventeenth to nineteenth centuries, as well as contemporary published materials of current Baptist and Baptist-related organizations and movements.

Some readers may wish to follow up with their own research of a particular theme, movement, or person within the larger Baptist narrative. Fortunately, in addition to books available at bookstores and local libraries and primary materials housed in archives, the technology-enabled twenty-first-century world allows easy and global access to a wealth of information. Many books are now available online via Google Books, and much primary material is also available on the Internet.

In order to further facilitate study of the themes, movements, and persons highlighted in this volume, interested readers are encouraged to do the following:

FIRST, READ ONE OR MORE OF THE FOLLOWING GENERAL BAPTIST HISTORY VOLUMES:
William H. Brackney, *A Genetic History of Baptist Thought* (Macon, GA: Mercer University Press, 2004).

Pamela R. Durso and Keith E. Durso, *The Story of Baptists in the United States* (Brentwood, TN: Baptist History and Heritage Society, 2006).

Bill Leonard, *Baptist Ways: A History* (Valley Forge, PA: Judson Press, 2003).

H. Leon McBeth, *The Baptist Heritage: Four Centuries of Baptist Witness* (Nashville, TN: Broadman Press, 1987).

G. Keith Parker, *Baptists in Europe: History & Confessions of Faith* (Nashville, TN: Broadman Press, 1982).

Richard V. Pierard (gen. ed.), *Baptists Together in Christ 1995-2005:*

A Hundred-Year History of the Baptist World Alliance (Falls Church, VA: Baptist World Alliance, 2005).

A. C. Underwood, *A History of English Baptists* (UK: Baptist Union of Great Britain and Ireland, 1970).

Albert W. Wardin, *Baptists around the World: A Comprehensive Handbook* (Nashville, TN: Broadman and Holman, 1995).

C. Douglas Weaver, *In Search of the New Testament Church: The Baptist Story* (Macon, GA: Mercer University Press, 2008).

SECOND, REFER TO TOPICS OF INTEREST ADDRESSED IN THE FOLLOWING HISTORICAL JOURNALS:

American Baptist Quarterly. Publication of the American Baptist Historical Society, 3001 Mercer University Drive, Atlanta, GA 30341 (www.abhsarchives.org).

Baptist History and Heritage. Publication of the Baptist History and Heritage Society, 3001 Mercer University Drive, Atlanta, GA 30341 (www.baptisthistory.org).

—The October 1992 (vol. 32, no. 4) issue of *Baptist History and Heritage,* titled "A Guide to Selected Baptist Bibliographies," provides an extensive listing, thematically organized, of Baptist-specific works to that time.

—The Spring 2009 (vol. 44, no. 2) issue has an up-to-date sketch of Baptist historiography. See Pamela R. Durso and C. Douglas Weaver, "So Many Books, So Little Time to Read: Baptist Historiography, 1979-2009."

Baptist Quarterly. Publication of the Baptist Historical Society, Britain (www.baptisthistory.org.uk).

THIRD, IF YOUR INTEREST IN BAPTIST HISTORY IS NARROWER IN SCOPE, READ VOLUMES THAT FOCUS ON YOUR AREA OF INTEREST, OF WHICH THE FOLLOWING SERVE AS EXAMPLES (AND ARE UTILIZED IN THIS BOOK):

John G. Crowley, *Primitive Baptists of the Wiregrass South: 1815 to the Present* (Gainesville: University Press of Florida, 1999).

William R. Estep, *The Whole Gospel For the Whole World: The Foreign Mission Board of the Southern Baptist Convention, 1845-1995* (Nashville, TN: Broadman and Holman, 1994)

Jesse C. Fletcher, *The Southern Baptist Convention: A Sesquicentennial History* (Nashville, TN: Broadman and Holman, 1994).

Wayne Flynt, *Alabama Baptists: Southern Baptists in the Heart of Dixie* (Tuscaloosa: University of Alabama Press, 1998).

Janet M. Lindman, *Bodies of Belief: Baptist Community in Early America* (Philadelphia: University of Pennsylvania Press, 2008).

Sandy D. Martin, *Black Baptists and African Missions* (Macon, GA: Mercer University Press, 1998).

FOURTH, REFER TO PRINTED PRIMARY MATERIALS SUCH AS:

David Benedict, *A General History of the Baptist Denomination in America and Other Parts of the World* (Boston: Lincoln & Edmonds, 1813). This volume is available online at: www.reformedreader.org/history/benedict/baptistdenomination/toc.htm.

William H. Brackney, *Baptist Life and Thought: A Source Book,* rev. ed. (Valley Forge, PA: Judson Press, 1998).

William Cathcart, *The Baptist Encyclopedia* (Philadelphia: Louis H. Everts, 1883). Available online via Google Books.

Joe Early, Jr. (ed.), *Readings in Baptist History: Four Centuries of Selected Documents* (Nashville, TN: Broadman and Holman, 2008).

H. Leon McBeth, *A Sourcebook for Baptist Heritage* (Nashville: Broadman Press, 1990).

William L. Lumpkin, *Baptist Confessions of Faith,* rev. ed. (Valley Forge, Penn.: Judson Press, 1969).

FIFTH, UTILIZE THE INTERNET TO FURTHER RESEARCH AREAS OF INTEREST.

1. For background information on many themes, movements, and persons, visit one or more of the following sites:

* Baptist History and Heritage Society–www.baptisthistory.org

* Center for Baptist Studies–www.centerforbaptiststudies.org
* The Baptist Index–www.brucegourley.com/baptists
2. Use Wikipedia (www.wikipedia.org) as a starting point for researching individuals and organizations; the reliability of the site is now on par with Britannica, although it should not be the only source utilized, or one's ending source.
3. If researching subject matter prior to the twentieth century, use search engines and/or the "Primary Sources" section of the Baptist Index link above.
4. If researching contemporary organizations, locate the official organizational site in order to gain an internal perspective.

SIXTH, READ THE FOLLOWING SPECIALIZED SOURCES FOR EACH CHAPTER, AND FOLLOW UP AS ACCESS AND RESOURCES ALLOW.

CHAPTER ONE

The early Baptist commitment to freedom of individual conscience, voluntary faith, religious liberty, and separation of church and state is critical to understanding the entire narrative of Baptists. For more detailed analysis of this theme, see Isaac Backus (David Weston edition), *A History of New England Baptists,* 2nd ed. (Newton, MA.: Backus Historical Society, 1871); James P. Byrd, *The Challenges of Roger Williams: Religious Liberty, Violent Persecution, and the Bible* (Macon, GA: Mercer University Press, 2002); Joe Early, Jr. (ed.), *The Life and Writings of Thomas Helwys* (Macon, GA: Mercer University Press, 2009); Edwin S. Gaustad (ed.), *Liberty of Conscience: Roger Williams in America* (Grand Rapids, MI: Eerdmans, 1991); and Lewis P. Little, *Imprisoned Preachers and Religious Liberty in Virginia* (Lynchburg, VA: J. P. Bell, 1938).

Early Baptists' commitment to the Bible understood scripture as authoritative in matters of faith and practice, and focused primarily on the New Testament. For more information, refer to seventeenth- and eighteenth-century confessions of faith included in Lumpkin, McBeth, and Early's source material collections; Weaver, *In Search of the New Testament Church*; James Leo Garrett, Jr., *Baptist Theology: A Four-Century Study* (Macon, GA: Mercer

University Press, 2009); and Beth Allison Barr, Bill J. Leonard, Mikaeal C. Parsons, and C. Douglas Weaver, *The Acts of the Apostles: Four Centuries of Baptist Interpretation* (Waco, TX: Baylor University Press, 2009).

Believer's baptism set Baptists apart from other Christians in Europe and the New World, and led to much persecution from state churches. Refer to related documents in Lumpkin, McBeth, and Early's source collection materials, as well as Benedict and Backus, and William G. McLoughlin, *Soul Liberty: The Baptists' Struggle in New England, 1630-1833* (Hanover and London: Brown University Press, 1991): 37-92.

The tension between the theologies of Calvinism and Arminianism occupied much of Baptist thought and action during the seventeenth and eighteenth centuries. Arminian theology characterized Baptists until the rise of Particular (Calvinistic) Baptists in England, after which Baptist theology found expression in both schools of thought and points in between. Among English Baptists, the earliest Baptist confessions of faith are General (Arminian) in nature: "Short Confession of Faith in XX Articles," 1609 (John Smyth); "A Short Confession of Faith, 1610" (Helwys and his followers); and "A Declaration of Faith of English People Remaining at Amsterdam" 1611 (Thomas Helwys). The 1644 First London Confession was the first to specify baptism by immersion. The hallmark confession of early English Particular (Calvinist) Baptists is the 1689 "London Baptist Confession" (a revision of the 1677 London Baptist Confession). Early Baptists in America, by way of contrast, did not formally part ways over Arminian and Calvinistic beliefs, and were less prone to pen their own confessions of faith. While Arminian Baptists found expression in Free Will Baptists during this era, many Baptists coalesced around the Calvinist-oriented 1742 "Philadelphia Baptist Confession of Faith," itself based on the 1677 London Baptist Confession. For these and other early Baptist confessions, refer to Lumpkin, McBeth, and Early's source collection materials. For an analysis of the Arminianin and Calvinistic strands of Baptist life, see Garrett, *Baptist Theology*.

Many individuals contributed to the story of seventeenth- and eighteenth-century Baptists. For a starting point regarding further information on persons introduced in this volume but not referenced above, refer to Cathcart, *Baptist Encyclopedia*; Edward C. Starr, *A Baptist Bibliography* (Rochester, NY:

American Baptist Historical Society, 1958; available online at http://www.baptist heritage.com/resources/starr.htm); Bill J. Leonard, *Dictionary of Baptists in America* (Downer's Grove, IL: Intervarsity Press, 1994); *Baptist History and Heritage* (www.baptisthistory.org/journal); and www.Wikipedia.org.

Baptists, of course, represented only one dimension of the religious landscape of seventeenth- and eighteenth-century Europe and Colonial America. For more information on the broader religious trajectory of this era, see: Thomas E. Buckley, *Church and State in Revolutionary Virginia, 1776-1787* (Charlottesville: University of Virginia Press, 1977); Kasper von Greyerz, *Religion and Culture in Early Modern Europe, 1500-1800* (New York: Oxford University Press, 2007); Charles H. Lippy, *Being Religious, American Style: A History of Popular Religiosity in the United States* (Westport, CT: Greenwood Press, 1994); Martin E. Marty, *Pilgrims in Their Own Land: 500 Years of Religion in America* (Boston: Little, Brown and Company, 1984); and Jon Meacham, *American Gospel: God, the Founding Fathers, and the Making of a Nation* (New York: Random House, 2006).

CHAPTER TWO

The era of missions, revivalism, and social reform (including abolitionism) played an important role in shaping Baptist life in the late eighteenth and early nineteenth centuries and following. Refer to General and Chapter One notes for obtaining further information about individuals and institutions of this era introduced in this volume.

The early years of the modern Christian missions era are explored in the following volumes: Gerald H. Anderson (ed.), *Biographical Dictionary of Christian Missions* (Grand Rapids, MI: Eerdmans, 1999); Stephen Neill and Owen Chadwick, *A History of Christian Missions* (New York: Penguin, 1991); and Norman Etherington (ed.), *Missions and Empire* (New York: Oxford University Press, 2008).

For more information on the Second Great Awakening, see: John B. Boles, *The Great Revival, 1787-1805: The Origins of the Southern Evangelical Mind* (Lexington: University of Kentucky Press, 1972); Charles G. Finney, *Experiencing Revival* (New Kensington, PA: Whitaker House, 2000); Donald G. Mathews, *Religion in the Old South* (Chicago: University of Chicago Press,

1979); Nathan O. Hatch, *The Democratization of American Christianity* (New Haven, CT: Yale University Press, 1991); Timothy L. Smith, *Revivalism and Social Reform: American Protestantism on the Eve of the Civil War* (Eugene, OR: Wipf & Stock, 2004); and William W. Sweet, *Religion on the American Frontier: The Baptists, 1783-1830* (Chicago: University of Chicago Press, 1931). For further research, a Second Great Awakening bibliography is available online at http://en.citizendium.org/wiki/Second_Great_Awakening/Bibliography.

Religion's relationship to and involvement within social reform and abolitionism and slavery movements are explored by: John P. Daly, *When Slavery Was Called Freedom: Evangelicalism, Proslavery, and the Causes of the Civil War* (Lexington: University Press of Kentucky, 2004); John R. McKivigan and Mitchell Snay, *Religion and the Antebellum Debate Over Slavery* (Athens, GA: University of Georgia Press, 1998); John R. McKivigan, *The War Against Pro-Slavery Religion: Abolitionism and Northern Churches, 1830-1865* (Ithaca, NY: Cornell University Press, 1984); and Smith, *Revivalism and Social Reform*.

CHAPTER THREE

The latter half of the nineteenth and the early twentieth centuries represent an era in which the Baptist faith took root in a number of non-Western countries and assumed modern organizational and ideological dimensions in the United States and Europe. Persecution characterized the life of Baptists in much of the world, while the American Civil War, the women's movement, and religious responses to scientific thought played a central role in shaping Baptists in America.

In addition to Baptist volumes referenced in the General Notes section, Rufus Spain, *At Ease in Zion: Social History of Southern Baptists, 1865-1900* (Tuscaloosa: University of Alabama Press, 2003) addresses social, moral, economic, and political changes in post-Civil War Southern Baptist life; Keith E. Durso, *Thy Will Be Done: A Biography of George W. Truett* (Macon, GA: Mercer University Press, 2009) offers a new examination of Truett; and James E. Tull, *High Church Baptists in the South: The Origin, Nature, and Influence of Landmarkism*, rev. ed. (Macon, GA: Mercer University Press, 2000) provides an overview of the Landmark movement.

For more information on religion and the American Civil War, see: C. C. Goen, *Broken Churches, Broken Nations: Denominational Schism and the Coming of the Civil War* (Macon, GA: Mercer University Press, 1997); Randall M. Miller, Harry S. Stout, Charles Reagan Wilson, *Religion and the American Civil War* (New York: Oxford University Press, 1998); the July/October 1997 (vol. 32, nos. 3 and 4) issue of *Baptist History and Heritage*, "Baptists and the Civil War"; and "Recent Historiography on Religion and the American Civil War" online at http://www.brucegourley.com/civilwar/religion.htm.

The African American Baptist experience and institutional advancement are examined by Evelyn Brooks Higginbotham, *Righteous Discontent: The Women's Movement in the Black Baptist Church, 1880-1920* (Cambridge, MA: Harvard University Press, 1993); C. Eric Lincoln and Lawrence H. Mamiya, *The Black Church in the African-American Experience* (Durham, NC: Duke University Press, 1990); and James Melvin Washington, *Frustrated Fellowship: The Black Baptist Quest for Social Power* (Macon, GA.: Mercer University Press, 1986).

The theme of women in Baptist life is explored by Jean E. Friedman, *Women and Community in The Evangelical South, 1830-1900* (Chapel Hill: University of North Carolina Press, 1985); Keith Harper, *Send the Light: Lottie Moon* (Macon, GA: Mercer University Press, 2002); and Keith Harper, *Rescue the Perishing: Selected Correspondence of Annie W. Armstrong* (Macon, GA: Mercer University Press, 2004).

The birth and development of fundamentalism is a complex subject. In addition to being the product of dispensationalism, reactions to modernism, biblical inerrancy, and the early-twentieth-century *Fundamentals* pamphlets, some historians focus on nuances within nineteenth-century revivalism and evangelicalism to further explain the phenomenon. For an excellent, brief summary article of historical interpretations of the origins and development of Christian fundamentalism, see Robert Wuthow, "The World of Funda-mentalism" (*Christian Century*, April 22, 1992), 426-29. The most detailed analysis of religious fundamentalisms (Christian, Islamic, Jewish, Hindu, and more) is provided by the multi-volume Fundamentalism Project authored by Martin Marty and Scott Appleby (go to http://www.press.uchicago.edu/

Complete/Series/FP.html for more information). Malise Ruthven's *Fundamentalism: A Very Short Introduction* (New York: Oxford University Press, 2007) summarizes, in effect, Martin and Appleby. In addition, George M. Marsden's *Fundamentalism and American Culture* (New York: Oxford University Press, 2006) focuses on the peculiarities of nineteenth- and twentieth-century American religion as birthed and shaped by fundamentalism. A bibliography of additional volumes addressing the subject of Baptists and fundamentalism is located online at http://www.wabashcenter.wabash.edu/resources/article2.aspx?id=10506, hosted by Wabash College.

A few additional notes require mentioning. Paul Keith Conklin, in "The Uneasy Center: Reformed Christianity in Antebellum America," in *The Journal of Interdisciplinary History*, December 22, 1997, 260-67, provides a brief overview of the dominance of Presbyterian theology in the antebellum South. Larry Crutchfield's *The Origins of Dispensationalism: The Darby Factor* (Lanham, MD: The University Press of America, 1991), provides an overview of the birth and development of John N. Darby's theology. Albert H. Newman, in *A History of Baptist Churches in the United States* (New York: Charles Scribner's Sons, 1915), 522-523, describes the 1905 St. Louis meeting prior to the formation of the Baptist World Alliance.

CHAPTER FOUR

From 1925 to 1963, religious persecution, Nazism, communism, and organizational growth challenged Baptists in Europe and throughout the world at large, while issues of race, civil rights, fundamentalism, progressivism, and institutional consolidation and friction characterized Baptist life in the United States.

For more information on Baptists of this era outside of the United States, see Justice C. Anderson, *An Evangelical Saga: Baptists and Their Precursors in Latin America* (Longwood, FL: Xulon Press, 2005); Bernard Green, *European Baptists and the Third Reich* (Didcot, Oxfordshire, UK: Baptist Historical Society, 2008); Pierard, *Baptists Together in Christ, 1995-2005*; Richard Steignmann-Gall, *The Holy Reich: Nazi Conceptions of Christianity, 1919–1945* (Cambridge and New York: Cambridge University Press, 2003); and

Wardin, *Baptists around the World*. Also see "Tommy Douglas: The Greatest of Them All," Canadian Broadcasting Corporation, undated; available online at http://www.cbc.ca/greatest/.

The issue of Baptists and religious liberty in America during this era found primary expression in the Baptist Joint Committee on Public Affairs (now Baptist Joint Committee for Religious Liberty, and online at www.bjconline. org). For a broad perspective of the work of the BJC, see J. Brent Walker's *Church-State Matters: Fighting for Religious Liberty in Our Nation's Capital* (Macon, GA: Mercer University Press, 2008). Also see James M. Dunn, *J. M. Dawson: Shaper of Public Affairs and Religious Liberty* (Nashville, TN: Historical Commission of the Southern Baptist Convention, 1987), and issues of the BJC's *Report from the Capital*, 1946-present. In addition, the American Baptist Bill of Rights (1939) reads in part: "Believing religious liberty to be not only an inalienable human right, but indispensable to human welfare, a Baptist must exercise himself to the utmost maintenance of absolute religious liberty for his Jewish neighbor, his Catholic neighbor, his Protestant neighbor, and for everybody else. Profoundly convinced that any deprivation of this right is a wrong to be challenged, Baptists condemn every form of compulsion in religion or restraint of the free consideration of the claims of religion. We stand for a civil state, 'with full liberty in religious concernments.'"

Baptists, race, and civil rights are explored by Andrew Manis, *A Fire You Can't Put Out: The Civil Rights Life of Birmingham's Reverend Fred Shuttlesworth* (Tuscaloosa: University of Alabama Press, 2001); Andrew Manis, *Southern Religions in Conflict: Black and White Baptists and Civil Rights, 1947-1957* (Athens: University of Georgia Press, 1987); Mark Newman, *Getting Right with God: Southern Baptists and Desegregation, 1945-1995* (Tuscaloosa: University of Alabama Press, 2001); Alan S. Willis, *All According to God's Plan: Southern Baptist Missions and Race, 1945-1970* (Lexington: University Press of Kentucky, 2004); and the Winter 1999 (vol. 34, no. 1) issue of *Baptist History and Heritage*, "Baptists and the Civil Rights Movement." A copy of Martin Luther King's "Letter From Birmingham Jail" is available online at http://www.mlkonline.net/jail.html.

Other helpful works addressing Southern Baptist themes include: John

L. Eighmy, *Churches in Cultural Captivity: A History of the Social Attitudes of Southern Baptists*, rev. ed. (Knoxville: University of Tennessee Press, 1987); Ralph H. Elliott, *The Genesis Controversy* (Macon, GA: Mercer University Press, 1992); and Bill Leonard, *God's Last and Only Hope: The Fragmentation of the Southern Baptist* Convention (Grand Rapids, MI.: Eerdmans, 1990). In addition, *TIME* magazine's coverage of the Elliott controversy ("Baptist Split," November 9, 1962) is available online at http://www.time.com/time/magazine/article/0,9171,829336,00.html.

CHAPTER FIVE

The late twentieth and early twenty-first centuries witnessed the majority Baptist presence shifting from the Western world to the Southern Hemisphere, while controversy and divisions increased in the United States.

For more information on Baptists outside of the United States, including the development of international Baptists in a global world, see: Anderson, *An Evangelical Saga*; Philip Jenkins, *The Next Christendom: The Coming of Global Christianity* (New York: Oxford University Press, 2007); Pierard, *Baptists Together in Christ 1995-2005*; Wardin, *Baptists around the World*. In addition, see *The Baptist Faith and Witness* series of the Baptist World Alliance (www.bwanet.org/default.aspx?pid=70) and the BWA's "2009 Statistics Report" (www.bwanet.org/default.aspx?pid=1179). Also see "Consultation on World Mission" *Hong Kong Peak*, March 1964 - http://www.abmhk.org.hk/thepeak-march196.html, and Andrew Rice, "Mission from Africa," *New York Times*, April 8, 2009.

The BWA's statistical report also contains current information on affiliated Baptist bodies within the United States.

The fundamentalist controversy transformed the Southern Baptist Convention and led to the founding of the Cooperative Baptist Fellowship and numerous other moderate Baptist organizations. Previously unmentioned volumes address these developments: Nancy T. Ammerman, *Baptist Battles: Social Change and Religious Conflict in the Southern Baptist Convention* (New Brunswick, NJ: Rutgers University Press, 1990); Nancy T. Ammerman (ed.), *Southern Baptists Observed: Multiple Perspectives on a Changing Denomination*

(Knoxville: University of Tennessee Press, 1993); Jerry Falwell, *The Funda-mentalist Phenomenon* (New York: Doubleday, 1981); Stephen P. Miller, *Billy Graham and the Rise of the Republican South* (Philadelphia: University of Pennsylvania Press, 2009); Paul Pressler, *A Hill on Which to Die: One Southern Baptist's Journey* (Nashville, TN: Broadman and Holman, 2002); Walter B. Shurden (ed.), *Struggle for the Soul of the SBC: Moderate Responses to the Fundamentalist Movement* (Macon, GA.: Mercer University Press, 1993); Walter B. Shurden and Randy Shepley (eds.), *Going for the Jugular: A Docu-mentary History of the SBC Holy War* (Macon, GA.: Mercer University Press, 1996); Walter B. Shurden, *Not An Easy Journey: Some Transitions in Baptist Life* (Macon, GA: Mercer University Press, 2005); and Oran Smith, *The Rise of Baptist Republicanism* (New York: New York University Press, 2000). In addition, Jeff Sharlett, in *The Family: The Secret Fundamentalism at the Heart of American Power* (New York: Harper, 2008), provides helpful historical back-ground regarding the rise of capitalistic fundamentalism. Also, Wade Burleson, in *Hardball Religion: Feeling the Fury of Fundamentalism* (Macon, GA: Smyth & Helwys, 2009), speaks to later divisions within Southern Baptist funda-mentalist/conservative ranks. Finally, Aaron Weaver's Master's thesis, "James M. Dunn and Soul Freedom: A Paradigm for Baptist Political Engagement in the Public Arena" (Baylor University, 2008) provides broader context for the Southern Baptist defunding of the Baptist Joint Committee on Public Affairs.

Helpful resources addressing some specific issues underlying the broad fundamentalist-moderate conflict in Baptist life at large include: Donald B. Cochrane, "Christian Opposition to Homosexuality," in James McNinch and Mary Cronin (eds.), *I Could Not Speak My Heart: Education and Social Justice for LGBT Youth* (Regina, Saskatchewan, Canada: Canadian Plains Research Centre, 2004—available online at http://www.usask.ca/education/people/cochraned/opposition.pdf); Richard Land on marriage (http://www.bpnews.net/bpcolumn.asp?ID=2439 and http://bpnews.net/BPnews.asp?ID=31506); the free market, capitalistic commitment found in much of contempo-rary, Western conservative Christianity is addressed by Rodney Stark, *The Victory of Reason: How Christianity Led to Freedom, Capitalism, and Western Success* (New York: Random House, 2006)—Stark, a professor at Baylor

University, argues that capitalism is inherently Christian in nature; Jerry Z. Muller, *The Mind and the Market: Capitalism in Modern European Thought* (New York: Knopf, 2002), a survey of historical Christian opposition to capitalism); and Richard Land's portrayal of public health care as "Nazism" (http://www.floridabaptistwitness.com/10836.article.print and http://bpnews.net/BPnews.asp?ID=31506).

Finally, the following denominational Web sites may be consulted for organizational perspectives (note: many international Baptist groups do not yet have a formal web presence):

American Baptist Association	www.abaptist.org
American Baptist Churches USA	www.abc-usa.org
Baptist Bible Fellowship International	www.bbfi.org
Baptist World Alliance	www.bwanet.org
Canadian Baptist Ministries	www.cbmin.org
Conservative Baptists	www.cbamerica.org
Cooperative Baptist Fellowship	www.thefellowship.info
European Baptist Federation	www.ebf.org
Fundamental Baptist Fellowship International	www.fbfi.org
General Association of Regular Baptist Churches	www.garbc.org
National Association of Freewill Baptists	www.nafwb.org
National Baptist Convention, USA	www.nationalbaptist.com
National Baptist Convention of America	www.nbca-inc.com
National Primitive Baptist Convention	www.natlprimbaptconv.org
Old School Primitive Baptists	www.oldschoolbaptists.com
Progressive National Baptist Convention	www.pnbc.org
Separate Baptists	www.separatebaptist.org
Seventh Day Baptist General Conference, North America	www.seventhdaybaptist.org
Southern Baptist Convention	www.sbc.net

INDEX

ABOUT THE AUTHOR

Bruce T. Gourley, of Bozeman, Montana, is a Baptist historian, writer, and entrepreneur. He serves as editor of the *Baptist Studies Bulletin* and as online editor of *Baptists Today*. In addition, he is the administrator and/or owner of a number of Baptist Web sites, including the Baptist History and Heritage Society site and BaptistLife.Com. Gourley holds degrees from Auburn University (Ph.D., History), The Southern Baptist Theological Seminary (M.Div.), and Mercer University (B.A. English, Christianity). Previously, he was the associate director and interim director for Mercer University's Center for Baptist Studies, professor of church history at Yellowstone Baptist College, and a Baptist campus minister. A longtime member of the Baptist History and Heritage Society and William H. Whitsitt Baptist Heritage Society, Gourley is the author of three books and numerous articles. His personal Web site is BruceGourley.Com.